THE FLORIDA EVERGLADES

Connie Toops

VOYAGEUR PRESS

To Fred and Sandy Dayhoff
who have graciously shared their love and knowledge of
one of the most beautiful places in the world.

Text and photographs copyright © 1998 by Connie Toops
First published by Voyageur Press under the title "The Everglades" © 1989 by Connie Toops

Revised edition edited by Todd R. Berger
Printed in Hong Kong

First edition   93   94   95   96   97   7   6   5   4   3
Revised edition   98   99   00   01   02   5   4   3   2   1

Library of Congress Cataloging-in-Publication Data available
ISBN 0-89658-104-7 (First ed.)
ISBN 0-89658-372-4 (Rev. ed.)

Distributed in Canada by Raincoast Books, 8680 Cambie Street, Vancouver, B.C. V6P 6M9

Published by Voyageur Press, Inc.
123 North Second Street, P.O. Box 338, Stillwater, MN 55082 U.S.A.
612-430-2210, fax 612-430-2211

Educators, fundraisers, premium and gift buyers, publicists, and marketing managers: Looking for creative products and new sales ideas? Voyageur Press books are available at special discounts when purchased in quantities, and special editions can be created to your specifications. For details contact the marketing department at 800-888-9653.

CONTENTS

UNRAVELING THE MYSTERIES

In the stillness of the dawn, fog shrouds the landscape, lending a remote and mysterious appearance to the Everglades. Before the first breath of wind swirls the mist, vague silhouettes of gnarled trees and roosting birds drift on a featureless gray backdrop.

In time, the sun peeks above the horizon. It bathes the grasses in a rosy glow and sparkles on dewdrops trapped in a spider's web. Mists give way to blue skies, but even illuminated in full sunlight, the Everglades are mystifying.

The region is half land, half water. Although tediously uniform in places, the area fosters tremendous diversity. This is a land of spectacular sights and subtle contrasts. As a naturalist, I learned that this unusual region may initially perplex visitors. For patient observers, however, the Everglades offer serendipitous discoveries.

During my first winter season, I lived fifty paces from the edge of Florida Bay, where bald eagles soar. I shall never forget the thrill of my first wild eagle, its immaculate white head and tail breathtaking against a cloudless sky. I recall canoeing from a maze of mangroves into open water at the precise moment a peregrine falcon dove on a flock of pintails. Among my neighbors were reddish egrets that skittered across the tidal flats and tawny bobcats with calculating yellow eyes.

Down the road from my little trailer, Mrazek Pond hosted beauty on a scale beyond imagination. For a few weeks each year, the drying pool teemed with fish and shrimp. Hundreds of ibises, egrets, storks, and spoonbills converged on the pond at sunrise. Troupes of white pelicans pirouetted in unison, dipping their beaks and savoring the rich seafood buffet. Snowy egrets tiptoed across the water like ballerinas in golden slippers, plucking minnows as they danced. Long-legged herons, their graceful forms silhouetted in the morning light, speared fish on rapier beaks.

The diverse vignettes of animal behavior that I witnessed began to fuse into a pattern of understanding, in much the same way that beautiful scenes emerged from the fog at sunrise. Each trip, each hour in the Everglades offered new sights and new insights. I began to identify with naturalist Charles Torey Simpson, who wrote in the 1920 edition of his book *In the Lower Florida Wilds:*

In my attempts to unravel Nature's mysteries, I have a sense of reverence and devotion. I feel as if I were on enchanted ground. And whenever any of its mysteries are revealed to me I have a feeling of elation—just as though the birds or the trees had told me their secrets and I had understood their language; that Nature herself had made me a confidant.

I continue to experience these feelings as I hike, canoe, and photograph in the Everglades. Over the years, I have explored some of the mysteries and been inspired to share some of the wonders. The Everglades will always be special to me, for they are the place I first met nature on nature's terms. Amid the mangroves or surrounded by a sea of sawgrass, I am at home—in harmony with a fascinating wilderness.

Mist shrouds a dwarf cypress forest at dawn.

DISCOVERING THE EVERGLADES

What are the Everglades *really* like?

Despite movie and television stereotypes, you will not find parrot-filled jungles with snakes dangling from every tree. The central, and largest, portion of the Everglades is a wet prairie, a golden ocean of sawgrass waving under sun-drenched skies. From a distance the prairie appears vast and lifeless. Up close, however, these glades are an intricate collage, full of life and surprises.

To really experience the Everglades, you must walk in them. Water will slosh over your shoetops, but you will not sink into quicksand. Alligators are not lying in wait to eat you, but you will discover captivating plants and animals. Amid the sawgrass you will begin to comprehend how these creatures survive in an unequaled environment.

As a naturalist, I led "slogs" (wet hikes) in which visitors shuffled with me through the water and mud. We stopped frequently to touch and taste, to sample the rich odors, to listen, to see with eyes and minds. The slogs allowed us to understand how plants, animals, weather, fire, and water acted upon and interacted with the land. We came to know the Everglades in a close and personal way.

One hot afternoon with about a dozen visitors in tow, I plunged into a spike rush wetland near Paurotis Pond. We paused several times to look and talk. Then I spied an interesting little spider on a blade of marsh grass. Its elongated front and back legs and thin profile provided such perfect camouflage that I was afraid the group would pass by without noticing. I halted to point it out. Unfortunately I stopped so abruptly that the woman behind me lost her footing in the slippery mud. I turned in time to see her teetering but was not close enough to grab her.

"Whoa," she cried as she backpedaled, her arms flailing in circles. Her sons, about seven and ten years old, had been walking at her side. She grabbed each by the shoulder in a desperate attempt to remain upright. Inertia carried her down, however, and the boys buckled under the strain. For what seemed to be a helpless eternity, the group watched as the trio plopped backwards into the swamp.

I rushed—as fast as one can rush in knee-deep mire—to their aid. Thankfully, the woman was fine and laughing so hard that tears trickled down her cheeks. "I've never had so much fun in my life," she giggled as we helped her to her feet. Covered from head to toe in mud, she joked that the park was now part of her. In her own way, the woman celebrated a personal introduction to the Everglades.

Yes, I could encourage visitors to touch a blade of sawgrass or dip their fingers into the cool, clear water. But in order for them to truly appreciate the place, the Everglades had to touch them back in a meaningful way. Only through this interchange do we learn to value and to conserve.

Much of the Everglades is a wet prairie, a trackless expanse of sawgrass dotted here and there with flocks of wading birds.

Sloughs, such as Sweetwater Strand in Big Cypress National Preserve, are slow-moving streams choked with cypress and pond apple trees, lush ferns, and air plants.

Thornbugs avoid predators by mimicking thorns.

People have touched the Everglades for centuries. Calusa Indians arrived nearly two thousand years ago, attracted by abundant fish and shellfish in the bays and estuaries. They still lived on the edges of the Everglades when Spanish and English explorers reached the southeast coast in the sixteenth century.

European contact was brief at first. Surveyors ventured only a short distance inland. Waist deep in water, they faced the flattest of flat lands, choked with razor-edged grasses. Rather than continue into this inhospitable region, they filled the empty spaces on their maps with the designation "River Glades."

Since the mid-1800s Seminole and Miccosukee Indians have made their camps on tree islands amid the sawgrass prairie. These hammocks are a world within a world. Shrubs, tangled vines, lush ferns, and orchids grow here in quiet profusion, the stillness broken only by mellow hoots of the barred owl.

The Calusas, and later the Miccosukee and Seminole Indians, used dugout canoes to navigate the many sloughs that meander through the glades. These slow-moving streams of fresh water are much broader and shallower than northern rivers. In some places they nurture thick cypress forests. The Big Cypress Swamp, a western section of the Everglades, is a mix of sloughs, narrow strands of cypress trees, and scattered pinelands. Alligators basking beside the dark water and broad-winged anhingas perched in overhanging branches lend a primeval appearance to these swampy waterways.

Along the coast, where saltwater replaces the fresh, tangles of mangroves stand in an impenetrable jumble. Mosquitoes are at times so thick that you cannot speak or breathe without ingesting some. Beyond these mangroves lie tidal flats where flocks of wading birds gorge on fish and shrimp.

Despite the mud and the discomfort of mosquitoes, this portion of south Florida has fascinated generation after generation. What is it about the Everglades that we find so alluring? The area is excitingly different—a place that seems fragile, but in truth, thrives upon flood and drought, fire and hurricane. It is a place of surprises, where resplendent reflections of a roseate spoonbill break the monotony of the mangrove jungle, and where out of the dreary grass, a hundred white ibises burst into flight.

The Everglades offer a tempting taste of the tropics. Bounded by warm oceans, with huge Lake Okeechobee to the north, the region resembles a tropical island tenuously attached to a temperate motherland. Of some seven hundred Everglades plants, 70 percent originated in the West Indies. Birds, too, show a strong Caribbean heritage. But mammals, reptiles, amphibians, and fishes are, for the most part, North American.

Curious contradictions abound in the Everglades. Southern Florida's shoreline was among the first on this continent to be explored; its interior among the last. Trackless wilderness lies only fifty miles from bustling downtown Miami. In the Everglades, "high" land is six feet above sea level. Yet plants on these rocky ridges differ from those in the lower marshes just as plants in the western United States change from mountain top to valley floor. Rather than the extremes of heat and cold common in most of our temperate nation, southern Florida has but two seasons, wet and dry. Year after year, cycles of drought are followed by periods of rain and renewal.

In no other place on earth do cypress swamps, sawgrass savannahs, and mangrove forests meet in such a manner. The Everglades produce a wellspring of wildlife, great and small. The region is so complex that no one vista or single creature can adequately symbolize it. Instead, the entire area has become a symbol of primal land that offers both raw beauty and spiritual refreshment.

In the Everglades you can still come face to face with an alligator or watch incalculable numbers of birds fill the evening skies. From spectacular sunsets to simple dewdrops that highlight each blade of grass, images of the Everglades lure us back for more. In this swamp we find vulnerability mixed with enduring spirit. In its reflections we may at times catch sight of ourselves.

Overleaf: White ibises at sunrise.

During the summer and fall, the Everglades are bathed in shallow water.

TRICKLES OF HOPE

Few places in this country have changed more during the past century than have the Everglades. In 1883, the New Orleans *Times-Democrat* sent an expedition to southern Florida, which was at that time as wild as any western frontier. After traversing the Everglades from Lake Okeechobee to the Gulf in a small boat, reporter A. P. Williams concluded:

It is a vast marsh interspersed with thousands of islands, with very few exceptions completely inundated, even during a very dry season. . . . They [the Everglades] are nothing more or less than a vast and useless marsh, and such they will remain for all time to come, in all probablilty.

"A vast and useless marsh." In an era of pioneering spirit, when capitalists viewed vacant land as opportunity, the phrase smacked of challenge. Little more than a decade after the words were written, rail service reached Brickell's trading post, now known as Miami. Develop-mania blossomed in south Florida during the 1910s and 1920s, obliterating native vegetation, draining surface water, and erecting architects' visions of tropical paradise.

In response, conservationists proposed a Tropical Everglades National Park, encompassing the southern tip of the state. Saving alligators and wading birds, however, was not high on the Congressional agenda. The park idea languished. Finally in 1947, President Truman set aside 2,200

square miles as Everglades National Park. In 1974, 570,000 acres of the Big Cypress Swamp became a federal preserve. Together these parks include an area slightly larger than the states of Delaware and Rhode Island. Yet the Everglades region stretches well beyond the borders of these sanctuaries. Everglades National Park and Big Cypress National Preserve protect only one-fifth of the original Everglades.

Everglades National Park was, however, a good beginning. Had it not been preserved, little of southern Florida's natural environment would exist today. But boundary signs do not insulate parks from encroaching urban influences. Brickell's trading post, when incorporated as the village of Miami in 1896, boasted 380 registered voters. Today the metropolis, which sprawls across eastern Dade County, is home to 1.8 million people. Florida's population continues to grow at an astounding pace—one thousand new residents move into the state *every day*. Some 4.5 million people live within a sixty-mile radius of Everglades National Park and Big Cypress Preserve.

Decisions about changing water patterns lie at the heart of most controversial park issues. Many northern and western natural areas are located at the head of pristine watersheds. In contrast, Everglades and Big Cypress receive their water—the vital ribbon that ties the package of life here—after it passes through two hundred miles of citrus groves, cattle pastures, and city sewage systems.

The Everglades watershed begins south of Orlando, where a core of low hills and rolling sand ridges plays out. The hills spill onto the lower Florida peninsula, a flat limestone seabed that emerged during the last ice age. The lower peninsula is bounded on the east by a narrow coastal ridge. It is broken in a few places by lazy rivers flowing into the Atlantic. Behind the ridge, the bedrock tilts ever so slightly to the south-southwest. Much of the rain that falls on the peninsula trickles, rather than rushes, across this plain (the original Everglades) into the Gulf of Mexico on the west and a broad estuary known as Florida Bay on the south.

When development began a century ago, no one recorded the precise patterns and amounts of water that coursed through this system. We do know that the headwaters of the Everglades watershed rose in a chain of lakes southwest of Orlando, very close to the present site of Disney World. The water cycle begins as towering thunderheads build in the heat of a midsummer day in central Florida. Fat, stinging drops fall in a gray curtain of rain. The showers move quickly across the flat land, leaving only steamy wisps of humidity and a few lingering puddles to confirm their passage.

The puddles converge into pools, which flow into winding creeks, and finally into larger lakes. Their names—Tohopekaliga, Hutchineha, and Kissimmee—imply that Seminole canoes first graced the sun-sparkled waters. At that time an energetic little sunfish could have wriggled its way during the rainy season through these creeks and lakes all the way south from Orlando to Okeechobee. Today locks on canals that were constructed to connect the lakes control the passage of canoes and sunfish.

"Remember the meander!" urged Marjory Stoneman Douglas, eloquent spokeswoman for the south Florida conservation movement and author of The Everglades: River of Grass. Mrs. Douglas, a spritely eighty-five years old when she addressed a group of my coworkers at Everglades National Park, described for us the Kissimmee River of her youth.

She spoke of a stream that flowed beside curving banks—banks overhung with spreading live oaks and festooned with garlands of delicate white moonflowers. The Kissimmee lollygagged across palmetto-stubbled savannahs on its way to Lake Okeechobee. When summer rains filled its oxbows, the excess surged into nearby marshes, home to fat crayfish, ducks, and sandhill cranes.

In the 1950s, Florida's water managers decided they could replace the Kissimmee's meanders with a straight course and reach Okeechobee in half the distance. So they gouged a two-hundred-foot-wide canal that shunts floodwaters directly into the big lake. Cattle graze where marshes once sparkled. With their habitat gone, wintering waterfowl and resident bald eagles all but vanished.

When the "Kissimmee Ditch" was completed, city sewage and pasture runoff torpedoed into Lake Okeechobee. Phosphorus levels skyrocketed and dissolved oxygen levels plummetted. Scummy algal mats bubbled up around the edge of the lake. Okeechobee's aquatic residents began to suffocate.

"Among other things," Mrs. Douglas reminded us, "meanders direct polluted water into purifying marshes." In 1986, thanks to her tireless crusade, a South Florida Water Management District demonstration project returned the meandering flow to twelve miles of the Kissimmee. The experiment is a success, and more of the old Kissimmee will be restored.

Lake Okeechobee's name is Seminole for "big water." At thirty miles long by thirty-seven miles wide, it is the largest body of fresh water south of the Great Lakes. Historically, the lake filled during the rainy season and excess water spilled into a bottomland tangle of knobby pond apple trees, woody vines, and head-high leather ferns along its southern shore. The swamp forest soil absorbed some of the flood; the rest coursed across thick layers of muck, derived from centuries of decaying sawgrass leaves. In the time before water management, our wandering sunfish could have continued south through Lake Okeechobee into the Everglades. Farmers, however, coveted this black soil and converted the marshes to fields of sugar cane, radishes, and oth-

Frequent summer thundershowers sweep across central and southern Florida, dropping gray curtains of rain on the Everglades watershed.

14

From Lake Okeechobee south to Homestead, winter vegetables grow on former Everglades marshland. Pumper trucks ply the fields, tapping shallow wells to irrigate the crops.

er winter vegetables.

When the weather riles up, as it often does during hurricane season, wind whips the surface of Lake Okeechobee into a fury of frothing waves. In 1926 and again two years later, hurricane waters ruptured flimsy dikes on the lake's southern edge. Two thousand people, mostly farm workers, were swept to their deaths. So engineers tamed Okeechobee by constructing huge levees around its perimeter.

The exposed muck farmland, covering an area equal to half of Everglades National Park, oxidized rapidly. During the first sugar cane harvest, the peat was fifteen feet thick. Now only one-third of that precious soil remains, and it continues to dwindle at the rate of an inch per year.

Canals and levees radiate from Lake Okeechobee like cracks in a shattered mirror. Former Everglades marshland, now subdivided into water conservation areas, serves as a storage reservoir. It maintains a head of freshwater in the glades to recharge the Biscayne Aquifer, which lies beneath in the porous limestone. Cities along Florida's southeast coast suck enough water every day from this aquifer to fill 20 million bathtubs.

In a dry season ritual, water from Lake Okeechobee irrigates the land. Each summer, however, giant pumps siphon excess water from the agricultural fields back into the canals or a water conservation area. Nutrients from farm runoff degrade water quality, in some places so severely that native plants die. Water flushes through a web of dikes, canals, and floodgates as the engineer wills, quenching thristy cattle and irrigating grapefruit trees. It is sucked away for fairways and power plants, bled off for growing cit-

ies, and finally carries back the sewage.

After two hundred miles of use and abuse, raindrops that fell near Orlando are belched through one last floodgate, into Everglades National Park. Into a park where wading bird specialist John Ogden shakes his head as he reports wood stork breeding success down 57 percent since 1970. Into a park where an estimated two-hundred thousand pairs of white ibis nested in the 1930s, but almost none nest now. Into a park where the Florida panther population teeters on the brink of extinction and only a score of female American crocodiles continues to breed.

An unparalleled ecosystem, an immense wilderness once teeming with wildlife, has been pushed to its last line of defense: a 2,200-square-mile park at the southern tip of the peninsula. It is a somber realization, but it hits home as I stand on the concrete lip of Spillway 12-A. This is one of four huge floodgates that direct water under the Tamiami Trail, from a management area into the park.

I gaze past the sluice, toward a dense stand of sawgrass where I watched a mother alligator carefully release her hatchlings from a nest of mud and plant stems. I glance west, where once I froze in my tracks as a tawny panther bounded into a clearing, then disappeared into the brush. A magnificent egret sails overhead on broad white wings. Its course is south by southwest into the park, the same direction this water will flow as it fans into the marsh.

I believe that accomplishments should be measured not in what we have defeated but in what we have allowed to survive. My eyes follow the water as it disappears into the dun-colored grass, where the real Everglades persist. To my way of thinking, the flow is a trickle of hope.

17

Sandhill cranes grub for insects in wetlands along the Kissimmee River. (Pat Toops)

Great egret.

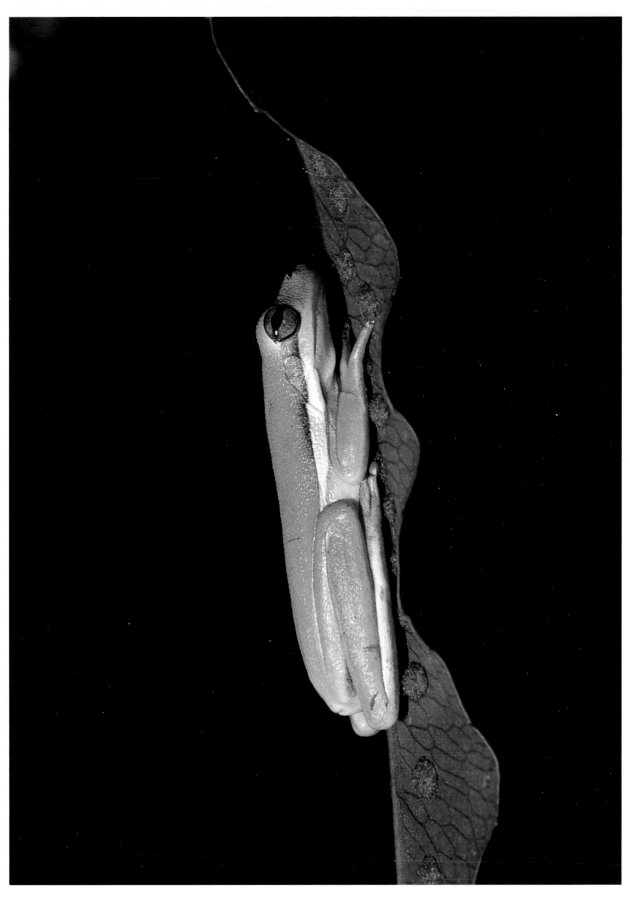

The Everglades are full of surprises, including well-camouflaged tree frogs clinging to fern fronds.

SEASONS AND CYCLES

The fifteen-mile Shark Valley loop road was originally constructed by oil prospectors. This narrow avenue penetrates the northern portion of Everglades National Park, the heart of the sawgrass glades. You may take a two-hour tram tour with a park naturalist, or you may hike or bicycle at your own pace, surrounded by solitude. On duty as well as for my personal pleasure, I have traveled this circuit more than five hundred times. Each trip provided an excitingly different glimpse into the River of Grass.

At the peak of the summer rainy season, knee-deep water inundates wide fields of sawgrass. The water is clear and warm, and if you stare at one spot long enough, you can gauge the flow. The valley's elevation sinks an imperceptible inch for each mile that you move closer to the Gulf of Mexico. If you dropped a feather into open water, it would float on the current about three hundred feet southwest in an hour.

Finding open water is not always easy. The shallows are crowded with dense sawgrass, a tough sedge whose leaves are set with tiny teeth, sharp as broken glass. Where the sawgrass thins, it is replaced by spike rush, a shorter plant with round green stems. In summer the bladderwort that grows among the rushes transforms these prairies into a buttery sea of blossoms.

Deer slosh through the glades, munching the succulent leaves of pickerelweed. They are totally at home in the water, and except for an occasional chase by a panther or grab by a gator, they have few enemies. Deer often browse in pairs. They periodically raise their heads to scan the horizon and cock their sensitive ears to listen. They glance reassuringly at each other, then satisfied that all is well, they continue to eat.

The white head of an egret appears here and there among the grasses. From June through November, when water is high and food is scattered, egrets and herons hunt alone. Their periodic squawks blend with guttural grunts of the pig frog, a southern cousin to the bullfrog. These shy amphibians live amid the floating lilies, seldom seen but easily recognized by their choruses, which sound like rooting hogs.

Summer heat and humidity are oppressive, and by midmorning puffy white clouds materialize on the southeastern horizon. For an hour or so the clouds play hide and seek with the sun as filtered light dapples the glades. The distant rumble of thunder draws an alligator's bellowing reply.

Cool downdrafts announce the storm's arrival. Gusts of wind and pelting rain bend the sawgrass nearly flat. The finest pulsating shower nozzle pales in comparison to an Everglades rain storm. Precipitation envelops everything in wind-driven sheets. The deluge usually lasts about fifteen minutes, complete with zigzags of lightning and bone-rattling thunderclaps. Then, as quickly as the storm descended, it moves on.

When the sun returns, it makes up for its absence by touching each drop lingering on a

Pearly-pink apple snail eggs adorn the sturdy stalks of pickerelweed.

Dewdrops dangle on spider webs amid the sawgrass.

Bladderwort blossoms float on a mat of feathery, air-filled leaflets. Each bladder opens periodically to absorb tiny creatures that live in the water.

22

leaftip or dribbling down a sawgrass stalk with a sparkling, star-shaped highlight. The air, which now smells incredibly fresh, is filled with the peeps and clicks of hundreds of marsh-dwelling insects.

Dragonflies sit atop the waving grasses. Their bulging, space alien eyes watch for passing mosquitoes and deer flies. Wings spread like a bi-plane, they face into the wind. When prey passes, they rattle into pursuit.

Beneath them float rounded, brown shells that once housed apple snails. These golf-ball-sized freshwater mollusks are the favorite prey of limpkins and the mainstay in the diet of the en-dangered snail kite. Apple snails glide under-water, gleaning algae from the stems of marsh plants. Now and then they rise to breathe through a snorkel-like tube.

Snail kites have a slow, buoyant flight, often hovering over the water. When a kite discovers an apple snail near the surface, the bird drops feet first and plucks the escargot from the marsh. Then the kite lands in a nearby shrub, pops off the snail's trapdoor operculum, and extracts the fleshy muscle with its curved beak. An adult will catch as many as sixty of these large snails a day to feed its brood of three hungry chicks.

Apple snails lay their pearly pink eggs above the high water mark on the stalks of pickerel-weed and sawgrass. Adults can bury themselves in the mud to pass a dry season, but when the young hatch, they must be able to reach water quickly or they will perish.

Snail kites may have followed the evolutionary avenue of specialization too far for their own good. Kite survival depends on prolific apple snail reproduction, which depends in turn upon abundant rainfall. The kite's specialized beak and weak talons are poorly adapted for extracting the meat of a small turtle from its shell, as kites have been known to try in times of snail scarcity. Kites dwindled to as few as fifty individuals during the drought of the late 1960s and early 1970s. Their present population of about five hundred is by no means assured of survival.

Life in the River of Grass is as intertwined as the dewy spider webs that dangle from the saw-grass. Consider, for example, the spongy mats of periphyton where baby apple snails seek refuge. The name of this colonial mass of plants comes from Greek—*peri* meaning "around," and *phyen*, "to grow." Indeed, various green and blue-green algae grow around the submerged stems of spike rush, bladderwort, and other glades plants, forming ropy clumps and blanket-like mats. One study found 281 species of tiny plants and microscopic animals enmeshed within or feeding upon this unusual community. Although easily overlooked, this complex mix nurtures many of the unseen, but vital, creatures at the base of the Everglades food chain.

Bladderwort is another of the glade's subtle curiosities. Beneath its yellow blossoms float feathery leaflets, adorned with minute, air-filled bladders. The plant has no roots. In order to ab-sorb trace elements, each bladder has a tiny open-ing that sucks in a swampwater soup of single- and multi-celled animals. The little creatures die and bladderwort absorbs their nutrients. Mosquitofish dart into the fringe of bladderwort leaves searching for midge larvae and water fleas. These aggressive little fish can eat their own weight daily in tiny invertebrates such as cope-pods and amphipods, which swim among the bladderworts.

The rainy season is a time of reproduction for most marsh dwellers, from minute members of the community, such as mosquitofish and apple snails, to the undisputed monarch, the alligator. Alligator courtship is in full swing by May, when the summer rains usually begin. Male and female alligators bellow to advertise their pres-ence and their position in a social system of dom-inance. Male gators have deeper voices than fe-males. They produce a rumbling bellow by arch-ing head and tail, breathing in, and vibrating air in their throats. The sound sends water droplets dancing into motion, surrounding the male ga-tor's neck like spray from a water fountain. In-dividuals recognize each other by sound.

Courting alligators swim and sun together for several days. On land, in what might be inter-preted as a tender gesture, the female allows the male to stroke her back with his front foot. In the water, they float with heads together, sometimes touching necks or noses. A male will submerge and blow streams of bubbles past a female's head. Couples test each other's strength before mating. Like playful teenagers in a pool, they take turns trying to press each other underwater.

By late June, females choose nest sites on the edges of tree islands or surrounded by open marsh. The gator uproots sawgrass and cattails, and by scraping mud, builds a mound that will rise above the summer's high water mark. She digs a cavity near the top with her hind feet and deposits about forty eggs.

Warmth from the decaying plants helps incubate the eggs. A baby alligator's sex is determined by the temperature of the nest during the first three weeks. Warmer eggs, usually near the top where hot sun shines day after day, become males. Cooler eggs from the bottom develop into females.

Raccoons relish alligator eggs and rip into unguarded nests. They crack the three-inch eggs and lap up the rich yolks. Since many female alligators remain with their nests, however, the raccoon may itself become lunch.

An attentive mother increases the chances of survival for her offspring, as I discovered firsthand. Along the Shark Valley Road, I noticed a pile of grass and mud at the edge of a small bayhead. The nest looked abandoned, so I parted the sawgrass to set up my tripod for a photo.

"Keek," squawked a startled moorhen. A six-foot alligator rushed toward me, gnashing her toothy jaws. As I scrambled back to the road, she planted herself beneath the open legs of my tripod, her pink mouth agape, hissing loudly. This gator was not taking motherhood lightly! I sat quietly, and finally mom backed closer to her nest. I retrieved the tripod and left her in peace.

Usually people have no problem when encountering alligators in the Everglades. Wild alligators are as anxious to escape as you will be to avoid them. Alligators that have been fed, however, lose their natural fear of humans and can be dangerous. Never swim in water that harbors gators, and keep at least twenty-five feet from gators that stand their ground as you approach.

A few days after my surprise meeting, I returned while this same mother gator was excavating her nest. Baby alligators can wiggle free of their leathery eggs and crawl out of the nest mound on their own. It is much easier, however, if mom is there to help. Baby gators make a nasal hiccuping sound. It attracts the attention of their mother just as effectively as the wail of a newborn infant summons a human. Baby gators begin grunting while inside the nest. If mom is nearby, she slithers out of the water and lays her head on the mound, listening intently. Convinced that time for release is eminent, mother gator claws into the heap of muck and decaying plants with alternating strokes of her front feet. In a few minutes she strips away the top inches of insulation, revealing unhatched eggs as well as a few babies that have squirmed free. They wriggle down the side of the nest mound into the sunlit water at its edge.

I was amused to see several tiny red-bellied turtles pop out of this nest. During a moment the mother gator was away, a female turtle had boldly deposited her clutch of eggs on top of the gator's, unknowingly insuring turtle offspring would also be protected.

As I watched from a safe distance, the mother gator grasped one of the unhatched eggs in her mouth and backed into the water, where she chomped on the chalky shell. Using just the right amount of pressure, she cracked the egg and a green-eyed baby gator swam unharmed from between her sharp teeth.

The lumbering reptile slid forward and swiped at the pile again with her clawed front feet. Inadvertently, she stepped on a black and yellow striped baby that tumbled out with the rotting leaves. It blinked, and none the worse for wear, toddled into the water.

Another of the leathery eggs rolled to the edge of the nest. Through binoculars I saw the shell ripple and a tiny black head pop through. "Umph," it hiccuped. "Umph, umph," answered the little gators already catching water beetles and minnows near the nest. The baby squirmed free and joined its siblings.

The excavation continued throughout the afternoon, and by nightfall nearly thirty babies clambered across mom's warty back or floated near her. The babies could live without her, but mom's presence offered protection from hungry

24

Pregnant alligators pile mud and leaves above the summer high water level. They lay about forty eggs in the nest. The eggs are incubated by warmth from the sun and the decaying plants.

Black and orange stripes camouflage a sunning baby alligator. (Pat Toops)

Female alligators sun beside courting males. In what looks to be a tender gesture, a male sometimes strokes its mate's back.

otters, raccoons, and herons. The little ones would stay near their mother for a year or two, doubling their size and honing their skills of survival. The lucky ones will claim territories in a few more years and raise families of their own.

The rainy season nurtures growth and reproduction, but daily thundershowers end by November. Then intense sun bears down from cloudless blue skies. The dry season is a time of testing for Everglades plants and animals. Winter breezes evaporate water from the ponds and sloughs. The searing sun is relentless. Water levels drop below the surface of the soil. Periphyton dries and crumbles. Deep cracks penetrate the parched marl. Day by day, as April drags into May, the remaining puddles shrink. Thousands of fish crowd into the putrid soup of warm, silt-laden water.

Among the best of the survivors are plucky killifish. Bass and bream, whose huge demand for dissolved oxygen can no longer be met by the noxious water, lie belly up around the edges of the pool. Gar hang on for a few more days, their long snouts breaking the surface in desperate gasps. Then they succomb. Vultures, boat-tailed grackles, and raccoons scavenge the puddles.

The killifish persist, packed like tinned sardines. It seems impossible that amid the bacteria of decay in the remaining pond there could be enough oxygen to support them. In truth, an inch or so below the surface, there is not. But killifish, and their mosquitofish cousins, are specialists. Their flat foreheads and tiny upturned mouths allow them to breathe from the oxygen-rich skim of water at the surface. It is constantly recharged by diffusion of oxygen from the air above.

Finally, on one late May afternoon, a bank of cumulus clouds builds over the Gulf. Instead of lingering tantalizingly on the horizon, as they have so many afternoons before, the clouds billow and darken and descend on the parched glades. Cool drops splatter on curled wisps of periphyton. In the following weeks, gray sheets of rain sweep in wide bands across the sawgrass. Every delicious drop is absorbed by the thirsty land. The drought has ended.

Hibernating frogs emerge from deep pockets of mud. They shriek in an ear-piercing frenzy, announcing the orgy of procreation that will fill clear new pools with jellylike strings of eggs. Out in the puddles that never completely dried, the killifish also sense the excitement of the season. Normally content to cruise their placid ponds, they now gather by the thousands where faster current from glades runoff feeds in. Splashing upstream like miniature salmon, they scatter once more to the far corners of the Everglades.

So it is that the seasons complete their cycle. The River of Grass once more stirs with the exhilaration of new life. Calamity is programmed into this annual ritual. Times of dryness are just as necessary as periods of flood. While some creatures merely survive the stress, others capitalize on it. They spread their genes to a new line of progeny that will in turn cope with next season's hardships.

Overleaf: Male and female alligators bellow during courtship to advertise their rank in a social system of dominance.

Viewed from above, an alligator hole is ringed by a privacy fence of dense willow shrubs.

WILDLIFE OF THE WATER HOLES

Toward the end of the dry season, sloughs that once spread across the glades like wide lakes are no longer there. The water table shrinks beneath the surface of the soil, below the grass roots. This would be a time of crisis for countless creatures that depend upon water as their lifeblood were it not for the chief engineer of the Everglades.

Tracks beneath the waving sawgrass reveal that the engineer's path is direct and deliberate. Clawed feet have pressed alternately into the mud. Their marks are bisected by the drag line of a heavy tail. The alligator has passed this way in search of a winter water hole.

Limestone beneath this engineer's belly is honeycombed with eroded cavities. Somehow the alligator senses water below. It rolls in the soft soil, flailing layers of silt and decayed plants aside with head and flanks until it hollows a depression. Typically these holes are six or seven yards in diameter and several feet deep. Gradually water from underground caverns in the surrounding bedrock oozes in to fill the void.

Damp mud thrown onto the banks provides an ideal seedbed for bay, willow, and cocoplum. These shrubs flourish and eventually encircle the hole like a privacy fence, but the alligator is seldom alone in its watery haven. Garfish and freshwater prawns swim beneath the willow boughs. Softshell and red-bellied turtles bask around the perimeter, as do several varieties of water snakes. Pig frogs grunt from the shallows; green tree frogs climb in the canopy. A green-backed heron hunts patiently at the water's edge. Now and then the gator harvests one of its guests for dinner, but usually landlord and tenants coexist in peace.

As wet weather haunts dry up, marsh-dwelling bream, bass, and tiny killifish migrate to the deeper water of the gator hole. Crayfish trek overland, traveling in lines that resemble miniature panzers bumping along over the cracked marl. Stinkpot turtles and warty old snappers, too, hitch across the dry glades in their slow-but-steady gait. Eventually, they reach the gator's oasis.

The alligator hole functions in the same way, though on a smaller scale, as water holes on the savannahs of East Africa. Both are microcosms, compact packages of life that reflect a larger domain. Both witness the dramatic interaction of predator and prey.

For a moment, imagine yourself in Africa. Glow from the rising sun bathes the fabled grasslands of Kenya's Masai Mara preserve, and in the cool morning air, a herd of zebras cautiously approaches the dwindling Mara River. One of the leaders shies nervously, realizing the danger in lowering its head to drink. But water beckons the thirsty herd. By ones and twos at first, they wade in and slake their thirst.

A lioness has pressed herself to the ground some sixty paces downwind. Suddenly the grasses part in a tawny blur. Zebras snort and scatter, but she has already pounced upon a colt

too confused to escape the streamside mire. The lioness grips the terrified animal's muzzle in a viselike death hold. In minutes, the throbbing battle is finished. The beast drags her prize into the shade of an acacia tree.

Now picture yourself half a world away, as the rising sun casts shadows to the far horizon of the Everglades. It is the hour when egrets and herons depart their leafy rookeries, fanning over the dry prairie in search of holes that still hold enough water to sustain bullheads and bream. By ones and twos, the gossamer-winged birds touch down in willows surrounding a gator hole. An immaculate white egret decides the coast is clear enough and glides to a landing at the far edge of the pool. Its presence reassures a trio of white ibises and a bold tricolored heron. Within an hour, two dozen squawking birds feast here.

All the while, a monstrous gator has lain motionless on a slab of limerock at the edge of the water. It seems oblivious to all but the warm sunbeam bathing its knobby black skin— oblivious except for the eyelid that raises just long enough to gauge the gathering of herons on the far side of the pool.

Nonchalantly, the gator pushes itself up on stubby legs and wades into the shallows. It plops down with a thud, as if the three lumbering steps were too much exertion. The herons glance in the direction of the splash, but quickly resume feeding. In a moment, the gator slips into deeper water.

Only the moss-covered turtle, basking on a waterlogged stump, notices the quiet ripple as the gator submerges. A while later, a pair of attentive eyes and the bulbous tip of a snout reemerge ten feet closer to the birds. A moorhen spies the gator, and recognizing it is on the prowl, paddles off in a new direction. Once more the gator's head sinks from view. Tranquil minutes pass.

"Aak-aak," shriek the waders as a dark torpedo explodes from the water. Instinctively the turtle plops into the water, and in a flash, the birds are gone. All of the birds except one, that is, for the gator has stalked well. It grasps an ibis in its massive jaws. The black behemoth slides back into the water, drowning all traces of life from the hapless bird.

When the gator finally resurfaces, a green-backed heron utters an agitated "tsk-tsk-tsk" call from deep in the willows. The alligator mauls its prey for several hours. It pulverizes the bird by crushing its bones between powerful jaws until the mushy white mass may be swallowed in one mighty gulp. With that gulp, the terror of death fades for a time, and one by one, the birds return.

As at the African water hole, the tension of the hunt has ended. For several days the lion will lie down among the gazelles and the gator will watch impassively as herons stalk fish at its water hole. Deer and raccoons, curious otters and mink will stop here for sustenance, and depart unharmed. The gator allows many more to survive the dry season than fall victim to its occasional hunger.

Alligator holes are wonderful places to study the ways wading birds coexist. Competition for aquatic food is intense. If all the herons, egrets, and ibises searched for the same food at the same time and place, they would spend so much energy squabbling that they would not eat. Instead, evolution has dealt each a unique strategy.

Great blue herons, blue-gray in color with mottlings of rust and white, are among the first to feast at gator holes. Taking advantage of a three-foot stature, they can wade in deeper water than their rivals. Great blues are solitary hunters. Not a feather quivers as they stand motionless, immersed to the knees, their scaly yellow legs blending with the surrounding plant stems.

A tricolored heron lands behind the great blue, near the edge of the pond. Its markings are similar to those of the great blue, but it is only half the size. The tricolored heron skips across the surface, flicking open its wings and jabbing with its beak. First left, then right, it weaves. Most jabs are rewarded with a wiggling killifish.

A few feet away, a little blue heron—equal in size to the tricolored, but a uniform slate blue— paces along the water's edge. Its head bobs from side to side in time to an unseen snake charmer's chant. The heron pauses momentarily to draw a bead, then strikes. For a second, a mosquitofish

Although alligators guard their holes, they share the water with otters, raccoons, snakes, turtles, and wading birds.

33

Alligators hollow depressions in the mud by flailing debris aside with their heads and flanks.

Ibises, egrets, and herons wade along the perimeter of an alligator hole.

flips between the black tips of its beak, then disappears in a greedy gulp.

A gangling wood stork parachutes from the azure sky, long black legs extended to absorb the impact of landing. It steps into the fish-filled water, bends over, and opens a thick, conical beak. Wood storks time their nesting to coincide with seasonal drydowns, when food is most abundant. To sustain two fast-growing chicks through the four-month natal period, a pair of storks must catch three and a half pounds of bullheads, mollies, and other small fish every day.

Stork beaks are sensitive to touch. When a fish bumps the waiting beak, it snaps shut in one-fortieth of a second, faster than you can blink. Is the fishing too slow? The stork steps forward, stirring the water with bright pink feet. If that doesn't frighten minnows into its primed bill, the stork will whip open its broad wings after each step, herding the fish toward its gaping mouth.

Ibis beaks differ in form and function from the wood stork's. The beak of an ibis is gracefully curved, making a handy hook to probe into the mud. Rather than spearing fish as egrets do, ibises use their bills as tweezers to extract snails and crayfish from below the waterline.

Splash! The statuesque great blue heron finally moved. One hour, one strike, one fat bream in the great blue's stomach. Patience paid off. The unlucky sunfish never realized those scaly stalks it swam between were actually the immobile legs of a hungry heron.

Seeing the heron's success, a great egret nudges closer. Almost as large as the great blue, this regal bird trails a mantle of lacy breeding plumes. Jab, splash, swallow — another bream disappears, this time down the throat of the egret.

The great blue raises its black crest and croaks menacingly. The egret retreats to a rock on the opposite side of the pond, shaking water droplets from its ruffled feathers. The egret, which threatens the heron's success, is driven away. Moments later an ibis waddles behind the great blue, probing the mud. The ibis goes unchallenged, as does the green-backed heron, which for the entire time has been perched nearby, darting minnows

Algae and floating-moss fern cover the shell of a red-bellied turtle.

and insects that enter its reedy shoal. Competition exists between birds of similar size and feeding styles, but overall, each finds its own niche and prospers.

Between meals, an anhinga rests on a willow branch above the gator hole. A primitive-looking bird with a black, egret-sized body, the anhinga clings to the branch with stubby webbed feet. Instead of stalking, anhingas hunt while swimming, poking beneath the lily pads for sunfish and bass. Anhingas submerge completely when fishing. Only their heads and slender, curved necks break the surface to breathe. This serpentine profile earned them the local name "snakebird."

Underwater, anhingas impale their prey with stiletto beaks. The problem is that once an anhinga skewers a wiggling bream, it cannot open its bill to swallow. The dark bird jerks its head and neck upward, trying to flip the fish into the air. This works for smaller fish, which the anhinga gobbles on the fly, but catfish and bream require more effort to pry loose. So the anhinga lurches to the nearest tree root, branch, or rock. Soaked to the skin, struggling to keep its balance, the awkward bird hauls itself from the slough and beats the fish against its perch. Finally lunch loosens enough to flip and eat.

One disadvantage of this fishing technique is the anhinga's inability to fly well after swimming. The birds must literally hang themselves out to dry — draping their broad wings in the sunshine and preening each feather meticulously to return the aerodynamic capabilites.

As the day shift departs the gator hole at dusk, night herons rouse from their roosts in nearby willow thickets. These stocky birds have shorter necks and legs than most of the other herons and egrets, but they employ the same stand-and-wait method of catching fish. Since larger competitors would chase them away during daylight hours, they hunt at night.

With so many birds, alligators, raccoons, and otters consuming them, it might seem that fish

Green-backed herons stalk quietly through the reeds in search of fish and crayfish. When alarmed, they broadcast a noisy "tsk-tsk-tsk" warning.

would be better off without as many predators. Although numerous individual fish are eaten, predators can never harvest all of a particular species from the pond. Actually, they remove fish at about the same rate the oxygen is depleted from the shrinking water supply. This allows the individuals that do escape a better chance to endure the stressful drought.

If you visit the Everglades during the dry season, you have an unequaled opportunity to observe the pulse of life and death around a gator hole. The Anhinga Trail, near the main park entrance, is an easy viewpoint. You may also hike through the glades to willow and cypress heads that shelter gator pools. Sit very quietly for several hours and observe the drama firsthand.

Approaching wildlife at a gator hole is similar to the stalking technique many wildlife photographers employ. It is a slow, careful process—a relationship in which the animal becomes accustomed to your presence and continues to do what it would if you were not there.

All animals, including humans, have limits to how closely they may be approached. The last time you stood in the back of a crowded elevator, did you feel as though your personal space was being encroached upon? In stalking wildlife, watch for signals that the animals are feeling those same jitters. Wildlife that feels pressed will flee. Animals along the Anhinga Trail are more accustomed to people than those you will encounter at isolated gator holes. Don't be disappointed if a few birds flush when you arrive. If you do not appear to be a threat, they will return.

I prefer to begin a stalk when an animal is occupied—feeding, preening, even dozing. If the creature stops its routine, I stop. Study a flower, pretend you are eating a leaf, avoid direct eye contact. If you carry a camera, take a shot each time you pause to acclimatize the animal to the sound and routine of your photography. Anticipate the lens you will need and begin with a fresh roll of film so you can be as quiet as possible.

It may take half an hour to maneuver into posi-

Stately great blue herons hunt by standing motionless until a fish swims within stabbing range.

In order to fly well, prehistoric-looking anhingas must dry and preen their feathers after swimming.

Common moorhens inhabit freshwater ponds and sloughs.

Curious baby raccoons search for insects and crayfish in the sawgrass.

From its perch in a pond apple tree, a green-backed heron peers at an alligator hole.

tion, keeping a low, nonthreatening posture. If the animal startles, freeze. Look away. Backtrack if necessary. Keep the welfare of the subject in mind. Your observations or photography should not disrupt its feeding or put the animal in danger.

Patience is sometimes generously rewarded. I have crept eyeball to blue eyeball with an ibis. I tagged along with a mother raccoon and three kits as they pattered through the sawgrass in search of grasshoppers and crayfish. Some of the most memorable sequences are captured in the mind rather than on film. As I knelt to photograph one of the raccoons, a dragonfly landed on a blade of grass just beyond my lens. The curious baby rushed over to grab the insect with its tiny black fingers, missed, and instead pressed its shiny nose against my telephoto. Of course, it was too close for a picture, but what a captivating look I received as those inquisitive eyes peered into my camera.

Another morning, my husband Pat and I were standing at the edge of a pool when we heard a commotion in the grass nearby. A female otter emerged, with a dead water snake in her mouth and a baby otter gnawing on the opposite end of the snake. We did not twitch. The otters, their brown fur glistening with a wet, oily sheen, chattered to each other and yanked at the rubbery snake, oblivious to our presence. We gazed at them for a quarter of an hour. At our feet, they twittered and rolled and ate the snake.

Finally mom sniffed us. Unalarmed, she led her youngster past us into the brush. Only then did we realize the camera had been around my neck the entire time and we had been too enthralled with the otters' breakfast to remember it.

Whenever I have been fortunate enough to witness (or photograph) a particular creature, my encounters usually end with an overpowering feeling of privilege. It is a compliment when an animal accepts my presence and continues with life as though I am not a threat.

In my philosophical moments, however, I wonder if photographers and film makers present an unrealistic picture of life in the wild. Nature films on public television whisk us from our living rooms to remote landscapes, into a hatching alligator's nest or a busy termite mound. We forget that some photographer waited in a blind three months for one memorable closeup. We are disappointed when we drive the thirty-eight miles through Everglades National Park to Flamingo and see only two egrets when the documentary portrayed two thousand.

Have we photographers, by taking the waiting out of watching wildlife, made animals appear more abundant? By getting close enough to show the stork's pink feet or the ibis's blue eye, have we pictured these animals as less shy than they really are? On film, one clear moment is captured for all time. In the wild, life is a blurred continuum.

There is no better place to witness Everglades life on the move than sitting near a gator hole—watching a black-masked raccoon peer cautiously from the grasses or listening to the delighted honks of ibises as they devour crayfish.

Fascinated, I lingered at one such hole late into the afternoon, long after the shadows become too dense for photography. The thought of disturbing that peaceful community with the clatter of tripod legs was the farthest thing from my mind. Instead, I sat quietly, absorbing the scene before me. It was a panorama to be relished in the mind and the heart, a private glimpse into the inner workings of the Everglades.

CYPRESS COUNTRY

The first pink streaks of dawn creep across the sky, and on the distant horizon, the humpbacked profile of a hill materializes from the darkness. Wait, this is south Florida. There are no hills. As the sun rises higher, it illuminates instead a thicket of cypress trees. Their height progresses in a perfect silhouette of a hill, from stubby dwarfs on the prairie fringes, to towering giants presiding over a deeper slough, and back to midgets again on the far side. The easiest places to see these cypress strands are between Ochopee and Forty-Mile Bend on the Tamiami Trail and near Pa-hay-okee along the main road through Everglades National Park.

Cypress country is a wildflower watcher's paradise. White-top sedges, false foxglove, and delicate spider lilies nod amid the wiregrass. Here and there, like glittering bursts of fireworks, wave the russet blossoms of butterfly plant.

It was in the cypresses that I first walked with Sandy Dayhoff, an environmental education specialist in the northern district of Everglades National Park. Sandy knows many of the flowers that bloom in the glades—botanically and by her grandmother's use of them for food or medicine. We sniffed the musky flowers of white tuber vine and shook the noisy seed pods of rattle pea, jumping back in laughter at their sound that mimics a diamondback.

Friendships are nurtured by walks in the woods and talk of birds or blossoms. Realizing my interest in such things, Sandy invited me home one afternoon to look at some orchids, which she and husband Fred grow as a hobby.

Fred and Sandy live in what is now the midst of Big Cypress National Preserve. When they began building their home, however, it was as Sandy says, "way out in the boonies." That afternoon, we bumped along a rutted dirt road past skinny cypress trees. Sandy pointed out the Gator Hook, a rough and tumble bar frequented by alligator poachers, and the site where gangster Al Capone once hung out.

Finally, where tree branches formed a canopy over the dusty road, we reached the Dayhoffs' gate. Their yard was a greenhouse without walls—spreading live oaks, wild tamarind trees, and red-barked gumbo limbos, draped and surrounded by hundreds of orchids and air plants.

Fred, a wilderness guide, and Sandy both grew up in south Florida and have explored nearly every alligator hole, heronry, and cypress strand from the Shark Slough to the Fakahatchee. Their knowledge of the region is the best kind, gained through years of personal observation. An outing with them becomes a pilgrimage of sorts, a visit to some special or little-known part of the Everglades.

"Let's go out on the airboat," Fred said one bright summer afternoon. When you live in the Big Cypress, an airboat excursion is equivalent to anyone else's Sunday afternoon drive. With a roar, we snaked south along a watery trail into the cypress country.

On an airboat in high water, you feel a boundless sense of freedom. The flat-bottomed craft skims over the surface, gliding across vegetation that pops up again in the boat's wake. Yes, airboats are noisy and controversial. Yes, prolonged use creates trails that are visible from the air. Recreational airboats are banned in the national park but allowed within certain sections of the preserve, including Lostmans Slough,

Cypress trees create shimmering reflections in Dayhoff Slough.

which we now zipped across.

The roar of the engine makes normal conversation impossible. Fred throttled back as Sandy pointed to some willows across the prairie. We trained our binoculars on the bird she spotted. Moments later, it lifted into flight. The white rump and lilting cadence of its wings were unmistakable. "Snail kite," we grinned.

Fred turned the airboat west, threading at half speed through ribs of cypress. He steered the boat by gunning blasts of air from a propeller past a movable rudder. There are no brakes. To reverse directions or stop, he would spin in a tight circle. At that moment, we were nosing through a sea of trees with just inches to spare between the gunwales and cypress trunks on either side. Fred's experience showed in a finesse few airboat operators achieve.

We wound our way into the most beautiful cypress slough I have ever seen. Frilly branches arched overhead. Air plant coronets adorned the regal trees, while lush green ferns robed their buttressed bases. The broad smile on Sandy's face and the twinkle in Fred's eye confirmed this was indeed a most special place.

We coasted to a halt, the sudden silence a stark contrast to the deafening airboat engine. "Does this have a name?" I quizzed. "Dayhoff Slough," Sandy answered quietly.

People who live close to the earth, as the Dayhoffs do, develop a tough physical endurance and a determined set of values to match. Their beliefs give them a strong sense of character and self-identity. How fitting that part of the Dayhoffs' legacy is this exquisite stand of cypresses, a one-of-a-kind place that will carry their name for generations to come.

Pencil-thin reflections of cypress trunks quivered on the surface of the dark water. Where shafts of dappled sunlight penetrated, we could see strands of water hyssop lilting on the clear current below. "The bottom is sand, rather than mud," Fred commented as he slipped into the waist-deep slough. He moved ahead, towing the airboat.

"Years ago we poled down here in a little boat," Sandy recalled. "That's when we cut this trail."

Fred walked the airboat through the largest stand of trees, not because they were too narrow to maneuver, but out of a sense of reverence. Each of us absorbed the tranquil images that floated by.

On the far side of the slough, Fred started the airboat again and we continued to a big gator hole. En route Sandy spotted a barred owl sitting sleepily on a spindly cypress branch. "It's always there," she said, as if greeting an old acquaintance. Fred told me he counted more than two hundred alligators in this pool during an exceptionally dry year. Now, at high water, the pond blended with the rest of the glades under a sea of spatterdock leaves.

Returning, we visited a lush spike rush prairie. The intense green of the carpet before us rose to a distant vista of cypresses, frosted with fluffy white clouds. Its undisturbed beauty and the silence were awesome. "How many people in the world know about this place?" I whispered. "Not many," Fred replied.

Other cypress forests are more accessible. Corkscrew Swamp, an Audubon sanctuary between Naples and Immokalee, protects a virgin stand of trees. Cypresses four to seven hundred years old and a hundred feet tall tower over the central portion of the swamp. On winter mornings, they stand in misty silence, as sunbeams filter through the bare branches. These are rugged survivors, their massive trunks scarred by lightning and their tops broken by periodic windstorms. Bald cypress, although a conifer, is not evergreen. Its needles rain down in a glittering golden shower each autumn and burst forth with the promise of new life again in spring.

A boardwalk threads through the preserve. From it, you can listen to the drumming cadence of a pileated woodpecker as it dissects a hollow snag for insects or peer into the haunting eyes of barred owls. Fallen cypress logs along the route are nurseries for ferns and basking posts for red-bellied turtles. The wide leaves of alligator flag wave over the dark water.

To birders, Corkscrew is famous as the largest remaining breeding ground for wood storks. Male storks, like knights in feathered armor, joust for nest sites in the huge cypresses. They

False foxglove.

Dwarf cypress trees dot the fringes of a sawgrass marsh.

fence with heavy bills, the loud clatter of their encounters echoing across the water.

Storks are stimulated to nest as winter water levels drop. Fish must fill the shrinking water holes in order for the storks, with their primitive method of angling, to catch enough food to raise young. The stout birds soar efficiently on five-foot wingspans. It is not unusual for them to spiral upward on morning thermals and glide thirty or forty miles to a water hole brimming with fish.

The problem, it seems, is that managed water levels do not always induce storks to nest as natural drydowns did. Water management tends to delay drying in some years. When this occurs, the storks begin nesting too late in the winter season. Spring rains scatter fish into the marsh, and storks abandon nests with half-grown chicks in them. There is less habitat for the storks to feed in now than years ago, another major problem.

Around the turn of the twentieth century, seven to ten thousand storks nested annually at Corkscrew. Everglades National Park also hosted sizable stork rookeries. In the late 1980s, Corkscrew attracts hundreds, rather than thousands, of storks. Everglades rookeries have stood nearly idle for more than a decade. If nothing can halt their precipitous decline, American wood storks will disappear shortly after the year 2000. According to Dr. William Robertson, dean of the Everglades National Park research staff, "The wood stork is presently the most threatened wading bird and probably the best single index to the health of the Everglades system."

The white ibis population is another bellwether. Once the most abundant wading bird in south Florida, ibis numbers have plummeted to about 10 percent of what their population was before European settlement, primarily because of loss of their wetlands habitat. These losses are ironic, since one of the most important influences in establishing Everglades National Park was concern for preserving its wading birds.

At the turn of this century, concern focused on great and snowy egrets. During the breeding season, great egrets sport more than fifty elongated feathers, called aigrettes, which drape about their shoulders like a lacy shawl. Snowy egrets display shorter versions of these frilly feathers. During the 1890s, ladies of high fashion began to decorate their broad-brimmed hats with aigrettes and the delicate pink wing feathers of roseate spoonbills. Suddenly a new occupation blossomed in southern Florida. Plume hunters ventured into wading bird rookeries to shoot "long whites" and "short whites," as the two species of egrets were known in the trade. One feather merchant alone shipped 130,000 egret skins to New York in 1892.

Egrets and spoonbills were shot while tending their nests. The slaughter left orphaned, half-feathered chicks to be eaten by predators or to starve to death. Even though other species were not in as high a demand for aigrettes, they shared rookeries with the plume birds. Constant disruption by market hunters caused them to desert their nests. Spoonbills and egrets were nearly wiped out, and most other wading bird populations declined.

The fledgling Audubon Society focused national attention on this slaughter, but initially the fervor pushed feather prices higher. Plumes were smuggled to Cuba, then via Paris or London, to New York milliners. For a time, aigrettes were worth twice their weight in gold. After the murders of two Audubon wardens and an extensive publicity campaign on behalf of the birds, aigrettes fell from favor. The whims of fashion shifted, and under protection, most wading bird populations increased to prehunting levels by the 1930s.

Few of the giant trees that held the waders' nests remain in the Big Cypress Swamp today. The name "Big Cypress," incidentally, refers to the vastness of the region rather than the size of its trees. The huge trees were cut in the 1940s and 1950s for their knot-free wood, which was valued for its rot-resistance. Train after train loaded with cypress timber steamed north during and after World War II.

Most of the trees in the Big Cypress today are quite old despite their dwarfed stature. Some believe these "pond" cypresses are a separate variety. Others claim they are bald cypresses stunted by the poorer sites on which they grow. Pond cypress needles do not flair open as widely and

Virgin bald cypress trees, some seven hundred years old and a hundred feet tall, tower over Corkscrew Swamp.

Disturbed water moccasins advertise their displeasure by displaying the cottony lining of their open mouths. (Pat Toops)

Wood stork numbers have declined alarmingly since the 1930s. The birds are now listed as an endangered species.

their trunks do not reach the tremendous size of slough-dwelling bald cypresses.

Cypress trees usually appear in even-aged stands rather than a mix of sizes. Even though cypress seeds will float for some time, the small brown kernels germinate only on moist, not flooded, soil. Once the seedlings sprout, they need time to grow before water levels rise again. This requires a prolonged dry spell if deeper sloughs, where the trees will ultimately reach their largest size, are to serve as seedbeds. Proper conditions occur perhaps once in a score or more of years.

The floor of a cypress forest is stubbled with knees, conical protuberances rising from the root system. Their role is uncertain. Popular theories include support for the shallow-rooted trees and oxygen exchange. They also provide handy places for ferns to sprout and snakes to sun.

Many people envision the Everglades as a land of snakes. Twenty-six species live here, but contrary to movie images, they do not drop from the trees onto passing visitors. Being cold-blooded, thus unable to regulate their body temperature, snakes enjoy lying in the sun on cool days. The best places to look for them are on logs or at the edge of the water. Nonpoisonous Florida water snakes and venomous cottonmouth moccasins are equally at home in the cypress country.

Young cottonmouths exhibit coppery brown markings, but older moccasins appear almost black. If disturbed, cottonmouths advertise their displeasure by shaking their tails and opening their mouths to show the pinkish lining. Two fangs, which inject poison, remain folded back into the roof of the mouth until moccasins bite.

Cottonmouths prey on frogs, fish, and rice rats. While some snakes kill their food by suffocation, pit vipers (moccasins and rattlesnakes) inject poison. This is an evolutionary advantage, since a snake's fragile teeth may be broken in the struggle to grasp fleeing prey. Vipers bite quickly and withdraw until the victim dies. Pits near each eye detect the faint trail of heat left by the dying animal. Flickering tongues interpret smell and taste sensations.

Cottonmouths sometimes rest on the flaring bases of pond apples, smallish trees that grow among the cypresses. Rough pond apple bark is draped with bundles of air plants, which thrive in the humidity above the slough. The pond apple, whose closest temperate relative is the pawpaw, produces fist-sized fruits in late summer. The fragrant, melon-colored flesh lures raccoons onto wavering branches to harvest the tasty globes. At this time of the year, raccoon scat, sometimes placed on logs as a territorial scent post, reveals masses of broad pond apple seeds that have passed undigested.

For the wild turkey, the black bear, and the Florida panther—all residents of cypress country—territorial markings and tracks may be the only signs casual visitors will encounter. Panthers are so scarce that even signs are elusive. In the late 1980s, only thirty or so survive. About two-thirds of the cats inhabit the Big Cypress-Fakahatchee region. The remainder roam hammocks and pinelands near Long Pine Key. Their decreasing numbers are a direct result of increasing human populations in southern Florida.

These reticent panthers, a distinct subspecies of animals elsewhere called mountain lions and cougars, are distinguished by a swirling cowlick in the tawny fur at the back of the neck and a distinct crook at the end of their black-tipped tails. They pounce from the underbrush on deer, wild hogs, and smaller prey such as armadillos and rabbits. Animals too big to be eaten at once are cached under leaves and soil. To catch even a glimpse of one of these big cats is exciting.

Seasonal change is more apparent in the cypress country than in any other Everglades region. In late winter, cardinal-colored air plant blossoms decorate the bare cypress branches and naked trunks make stark silhouettes against the setting sun. A few months later, the same forest is haloed by soft green foliage. Anoles, commonly called chameleons, scamper across the stringy cypress bark. Their green backs are as bright as the new spring buds. Here, seasons change like the colors of the anole—from brown to green and back to brown again. Despite varying outward appearances, however, the cypress forest is an enduring home to an array of fascinating plants and animals.

White ibises were once abundant in the Everglades. Due to the development of surrounding wetlands, Everglades National Park now hosts only a fraction of its former ibis population.

Hammock growing space is limited. Strangler figs begin life on the limb of a host tree. The fig's roots eventually encircle the host in a viselike death grip.

ISLANDS
IN THE STREAM

The flight pattern for passenger jets landing at Miami International Airport circles in a long, slow descent over the Everglades. The final leg cuts directly across Shark Slough. Travelers who peer at the glades from several thousand feet above see a green flotilla of tree islands sailing through a sea of golden sawgrass.

If these hammocks were ships, their pointed bows would all face downstream, south by southwest toward the Gulf. In reality, the tree islands are moored fast to numerous rocky outcrops that emerge from the wetlands. These islets vary in size, the majority ranging from one to ten acres. During times of high water, the current parts at the head of each gnarled outcrop, swirls along the side, and drops minute bits of silt where the waters rejoin downstream. Over the centuries, these muck deposits have enlarged the hammocks, giving them a characteristic teardrop shape.

No one can say for certain which of the more than one hundred species of broadleaved trees native to the Everglades first populated these hammocks several thousand years ago. Among the pioneers, no doubt, were bay trees and hardy cocoplum shrubs, whose large seeds float with the current. Once nestled in a pocket of humus on the edge of a limestone island, the seeds sprouted, their fingerlike roots twining through subsurface crannies.

Birds sat in the spreading branches of these young trees, their seed-laden droppings falling on the thin layer of decayed leaves and humus that covered the knobby limestone. Seeds of other trees and shrubs arrived on the wind. Oaks, myrtles, and laurels sprang up amid the pioneering bays and cocoplums. As the hammock forest grew, its canopy began to block the harsh sunlight and hold in moisture, protecting the delicate plants inside much as a greenhouse does. Ferns and orchids luxuriated in the humid air.

Centuries passed and the cloak of leaf litter, called duff, thickened. Raindrops percolated through this decaying humus, absorbing weak organic acids. As the runoff slid across the rock islands and dripped off their edges, caustic water dissolved the limestone. In time a moat ringed each outcrop. Where acid water puddled in the midst of the tree islands, it pocked the rock in a karst pattern of large and small solution holes. During wetter times, the moats and solution holes hold standing water. Fire may rage across the sawgrass plain, but the damp perimeter and dripping humidity inside a hammock prevent the flames from entering.

Hammocks are also found within pine forests. From the air, it is easy to pick out dense circular patches of green foliage amid the more open pinelands. Here, as in the sawgrass glades, fire has been excluded for years, allowing shade-tolerant hardwood trees and shrubs to proliferate. These hammocks are also pitted by solution holes and in all but the driest times create their own fire protection by trapping high humidity.

Overleaf: From the air, the characteristic teardrop shape of a hammock stands in sharp contrast to the sea of golden sawgrass that surrounds it.

53

Tree snails are active during the rainy season, gorging themselves on lichens.

Countless ants and beetles roam beneath leaves that are trapped in the cupped bases of air plants.

Hammocks vary slightly from one end of the Everglades to the other. On the north, they contain many temperate species. Southward, especially along the coast, tropical trees and shrubs prevail. Hammocks on the Keys are drier, thus lacking the lush undergrowth and moisture-loving air plants. Pigeon plum, gumbo limbo, drab Jamaica dogwood, and mahogany are the principal components. White-crowned pigeons feed on fruits in the forest canopy while an occasional gray squirrel scampers busily between branches and forest floor.

A hammock's distinctive outline is unmistakable from the air, but to best partake of this world of dense greenery, explore at ground level. The experience of walking through the vast, sunlit —and usually wet—glades, then stepping up on-to a cool, dry plateau where views seldom exceed ten yards is one of the greatest contrasts in the Everglades.

After you have sloshed through the moat and climbed onto the edge of the hammock, you may have to fight through a tangle of dense bushes and thorny vines to enter the inner sanctum. Once inside, leaves and branches brush your shoulders as you thread between the closely spaced saplings. The skunky odor of stopper, a common shrub, wafts through the damp air. Your steps are slow and careful, as you at once watch the ground for solution holes half-hidden under the crunchy leaf litter and look ahead to dodge ubiquitous spider webs.

Invariably you will walk into an unseen web, usually the strong, spreading strands of a golden orb weaver. The clammy silk envelops your cheeks and instinctively you step back to swab your face. Inches above, the gentle half-dollar-sized spider scrambles to safety before it is en-gulfed in trailing filaments of its own sticky snare.

Within the hammock, your eyes focus on near-by objects—the showy butterflies, the bulbous-based orchids that cling to furrowed live oak bark, the living jewels known as tree snails.

Liguus (banded) tree snails—whose conical shells are decorated with whorls of brown, deli-

Purple flowers of the stiff-leaved air plant are borne on showy red bracts.

Gumbo limbo, a hammock tree, is easily identified by its peeling red bark.

cate green etchings, and yellow highlights—glide across smooth-barked fig, wild tamarind, and pigeon plum trees. They scrape algae and lichen into their mouths with rasping tongues called radulas.

Similar snails reside in Cuba and Hispaniola, an observation that lends to speculation that ancestors of the Florida snails may have arrived attached to floating logs. They dispersed into hammocks of the Keys and Everglades. The Florida snails bred and interbred, giving rise to more than fifty distinctive color forms. Some colonies were more isolated than others, thus a few patterns are known from only one hammock or small cluster of tree islands.

Unfortunately, many hammocks in Miami and the Keys were casualties of development. Erwin Winte, one of the first park rangers in the Everglades, realized the snail's homes were disappearing and collected color forms from many areas before they fell victim to the bulldozer's blade. He relocated more than two dozen threatened *Liguus* varieties, half of which are now extinct in

their native hammocks, into Everglades National Park.

Summer visitors are most likely to encounter active tree snails, since the moisture-sensitive mollusks feed after rainshowers. They glide across damp bark on a rippling foot muscle, covering at a snail's pace about twenty-five feet a day. Ligs mate at the end of the summer in a twining ritual that lasts up to forty-eight hours. Being hermaphrodites (each individual possesses both male and female organs), both leave the encounter pregnant. Several days afterward, the egg-laden snails descend to the ground for one of the few times in their four- to eight-year life spans.

On an August afternoon, I followed Fred and Sandy Dayhoff into a hammock on the northeast edge of Lostmans Slough. Within moments, each had spotted tree snails laying eggs. "They dig down into the leaf litter," Fred explained, pointing to a pink-tipped shell buried near the base of a wild tamarind tree.

He scraped away some of the debris so I could

see the glistening pink eggs in the cavity beneath the snail's body. Oblong and no larger than the tip of my little finger, the eggs shimmered with the luster of fine pearls. Nests contain from fifteen to fifty eggs, which Fred explained remain in the ground throughout the winter.

"The babies hatch after the first spring shower," Sandy added. The tiny snails, which she called "buttons," grow quickly, adding two or three whorls to their shells during the summer.

Tree snails gorge during the rainy season, then attach themselves with tough mucous to wait out the winter on a tree branch or trunk. The torpid snails snooze within their weather-tight shells, awakening again when summer rains dissolve the seal.

Hammocks are lush botanical showplaces, home to a dazzling display of plant diversity. Since growing space in the fertile soil is at a premium, some plants have developed ways to elevate themselves above this competition. The strangler fig begins life as a seed that falls from bird droppings into the crevice of a tree branch. Able to absorb moisture from rain and humidity, the fig sapling flourishes high overhead. But as it grows, it sends out aerial roots that insidiously wrap around the host on the way down. Once roots entrench in the duff, the fig grows rapidly. Within a few years its grappling roots will strangle the host tree.

Ferns, orchids, and bromeliads—plants that look like pineapple tops—respond to the shortage of growing space by living piggy back on trees and shrubs. The name *epiphyte* (plant growing upon plant) suggests that unlike parasites, bromeliads take nothing from their host except support. Air plants, as they are commonly called, catch rain in their cupped bases and cull moisture from the humidity through specialized scales on their leaves. They obtain nutrients from decaying leaves, dust, and animal droppings that accumulate at the base of their stalks.

Peeking into the rosette of an air plant on a hammock reveals a world within a world. Beneath the leaf bits, bull ants and hard-shelled black beetles roam in search of tinier insects. Spiders and hook-tailed scorpions lie ready to ambush these creepers and crawlers. Tree frogs,

attracted by the moisture in the clasping sheaths of the lower leaves, gobble up the insects but are in turn devoured by slinky green snakes that patrol the forest canopy.

Bromeliads bloom in the spring, their minute purple flowers unnoticed at a distance because of the showier red bracts on which they are borne. Nectar in the tubular flowers attracts both butterflies and hummingbirds.

Among the most familiar of the hammock butterflies is the black and yellow zebra. This slow-flying species, with wings twice as long as wide, seldom flutters far from passion vine. It is the only plant upon which the caterpillars feed. Yellow eggs—each shaped like an ear of corn but only the size of a pinhead—are attached singly on the tender leaves near the end of the vine.

Broods of zebra butterflies rest together at night in the shrubby cover of a hammock. Before dusk on a winter evening, park volunteer Donna Morris led me into Redd Hammock, where she had recently discovered a zebra roost. Donna paused a few feet from a tangled, leafless vine. Had she not stopped, I would never have noticed the half dozen butterflies clinging together in the gathering darkness.

By day, though the zebra's listless flight would seem to make it an easy target for songbirds, it flutters unmolested. Passion vine gives zebras a disagreeable taste. Birds learn that black and yellow striped butterflies are unpalatable and avoid them. At dawn and dusk, when roosting colonies would seem vulnerable, the bold color pattern once again protects them. Dark folded wings melt into the night sky. Narrow yellow bars, which angle away from the zebra's body, continue the contorted pattern of its twig-studded perch. Individual zebras blend imperceptibly with their background.

The absolute master of camouflage in the hammock is the three-inch bark mantis. It lurks on the urn-shaped bases of stately royal palm trees. Palm trunks sport crusty growths of grayish lichens, plants that are combinations of algae and fungi. The bark mantis mimics these blotchy patterns exactly, lying motionless until an ant or beetle scurries past. Then, with lightning swiftness, the mantis pounces and captures its prey

Masterfully camouflaged, a bark mantis blends with lichens on a royal palm trunk.

The zebra belongs to a family of tropical butterflies. Most predators ignore these delicate butterflies because they have a disagreeable taste.

between barbed forelegs.

Hammocks are so diverse and full of life that it takes extra time to absorb their complex beauty. Some years ago I had such an opportunity when I spent the night on a hammock in Shark Slough. I was one of three naturalists scouting a place to lead visitors on overnight backpacking trips.

After several sweaty hours of stumbling across jagged pinnacle rock in the open prairie, we reached the welcoming shade of the hammock. As we pitched our tents, we discovered we were not the first to inhabit this island. Old bottles and pottery shards dappled the leaf litter. Near a clearing in the midst of the island lay a cracked iron cooking pot and the rusting remains of a treadle sewing machine, sure signs that at one time this was the home of Miccosukee Indians.

Miccosukees belong to the Creek Nation and arrived in south Florida in the mid-1800s. They lived in thatch-roofed shelters, or chickees, built on larger hammocks. Miccosukees traveled about in dugout canoes made from cypress logs, occasionally taking trade goods such as animal pelts and plumes to coastal outposts. There they obtained the sewing machines and colorful calico from which Miccosukee women made the brightly patterned shirts and skirts that became their trademark.

The camp on this hammock would have included four or five open-sided chickees, one for cooking, one for dining and storage, and the remainder for sleeping. When the Indians were not resting, their raised platform beds would be cleared and used as work tables. In the dim light of late afternoon, I could almost smell the smoky fire that heated water in the soot-blackened pot and anticipate the supper of warm, moist fry bread served with sofkee, a thin porridge made from corn grits.

"Who-who-who-whoall." The soft hoot of a barred owl in the branches overhead jarred me into the present once more. Many Miccosukee folk legends involve o-pa-gee, the owl. Pairs of these inquisitive birds inhabit most of the larger hammocks in the region.

Outside a breeze rattled through the sawgrass, but here within the hammock it was still. Cardinals and towhees signaled the end of another day with a pleasant banter of soft whistles and settled into their shrubby hides for the night. On the evening's damp air came a chorus of unseen songsters. I recognized the cricket's monotone and the squeaky notes of the tree frog, but the rest were left to imagination. The golden flickering of lightning bugs suggested it was time for tired hikers to turn in.

Before dawn the cushioning power of my foam sleeping pad played out. No matter which way I turned, a hard knob of pinnacle rock poked my ribs. Not wishing to awaken the others, I slipped out of the tent and tiptoed to the edge of the hammock. Through a break in the leafy canopy, the black sky shimmered with more stars than I had ever seen before, their clarity and brightness undimmed by artifical light. A sparkling meteorite streaked across the eastern horizon, where a sliver of moon waned. And in the distance a pair of owls serenaded each other.

It was a peaceful view, as I watched the sun come up from my cozy retreat. For many of the Everglades plants and animals, the hammock is just that—a sheltering homeplace, a refuge from the rigors of searing sun or mucky wetness in the surrounding marsh. As later that morning I rolled my tent and refluffed the leaf litter beneath it, I did so with new insight into the complex tree island community.

Periodic fires maintain a balance between shady hammocks and sun-loving pine forests.

FORESTS BORN OF FLAMES

Park volunteer Vic Morris grew up in Homestead, Florida. Years before the establishment of Everglades National Park, young Vic would ride with his father on trips into Miami. Along that thirty-mile stretch of U.S. Highway 1 in the 1930s, they might encounter only one or two other cars. Instead of today's houses and shopping malls, Vic saw endless ranks of feathery pines, their lean brown trunks rising above jagged palmetto fronds.

South Florida pines, a gnarly limbed subtropical variety of slash pine, occupy the Atlantic Coastal Ridge. The ridge is a narrow band of oolitic limestone that extends along Florida's east coast from Fort Lauderdale to Homestead, then swings southwest into the park. It ends in a rocky shield known as Long Pine Key.

This "high pineland," as early residents called it, rose as much as twenty feet above sea level at its northern end. It is the most desirable building substrate on the southeast coast. Glance at a Florida map. Within Vic's lifetime, what was pine and palmetto has become an unbroken urban strip from Pompano to Princeton. Today the last sizable pineland remnants are preserved in Everglades National Park. Scattered islands of pine also survive throughout the Big Cypress Swamp.

Miami oolite is jagged rock, eroded by the same combination of rainwater and organic acids that gnaws moats around hammocks. The pineland rim, studded with knife-edged spires and Swiss-cheese holes, is painfully slow to hike across. It would seem inhospitable to most plants, especially after fire consumes the leaf litter and exposes the barren rock. Yet pine trees, palmettos, and a host of endemic herbs thrive here.

To understand how they persist, study the exposed roots of a toppled pine. In life these anchors spread wide, their curling fingers spiraling into moist cavities in the honeycombed rock. Their grasp was tight—so tight in fact that when the tree finally fell, its roots pried up huge chunks of stone. These hunks of warty oolite remain imbedded in the roots until they decay, a natural headstone that testifies to the tree's tenaciousness.

Were it not for fire, the understory of the sun-loving slash pine forest would eventually be invaded by shade-tolerant hammock species. Before the arrival of the first people in southern Florida, lightning ignited periodic fires, most during summer thunderstorms. Slash pine and saw palmetto have multilayered bark. Creeping ground fires singe the outside (like a match held to a tightly rolled newspaper), but the inner cambium remains protected. The flames consume grasses and low bushes, fertilizing the soil with their ashes and opening the forest floor to sunlight. Seeds drop from slash pine cones onto this welcoming bed and germinate quickly.

Young pines put much of their initial energy into root growth, sending a strong tap threading

through crevices in the lime rock. For the first several growing seasons, needles of these "grass stage" seedlings cluster tightly around the tender buds. Amazingly, young slash pines can lose up to half their needles to scorching heat, but as long as the bud is protected, they withstand the flames.

Coontie, like many of the other pinelands plants, grows from a tuberous rootstalk. Fire may consume its plume-like leaves, but starches and moisture stored within the stocky base combine to push out new foliage a week or two after the fire's passage. The Indians regarded this fleshy cycad as manna, grubbing the rootstalks from between the rocks and extracting their starchy flour.

Wet season fires pose little threat to plants or animals. They burn in irregular, mosaic patterns, allowing quail and rabbits to scamper away from the flames. Turtles, lizards, and snakes slip into holes in the oolite while the fire sweeps overhead. Swallow-tailed kites and red-shouldered hawks swoop into the smoke, snatching grasshoppers and other large insects as they hop from the flames. The burned areas green quickly after summer fires pass, luring deer to graze on succulent new vegetation.

Fires during the dry season (most of which are caused by people) have more disastrous results. Without moisture, peat soil burns. Smoldering flames creep through pockets of soil in the limestone, consuming pine taproots and coontie tubers. Unchecked, they lap onto hammocks, destroying the root network. Trees that may have grown here for a century or more topple within hours after invasion by the underground fires.

Since south Florida's water is so strictly managed, the area is no longer a truly natural ecosystem. Because water levels are generally lower now than at the turn of the century, fires are potentially more damaging. Everglades became the first national park to employ "prescribed" fires. These are closely supervised fires which are permitted to burn during favorable moisture conditions. They perpetuate fire-dependent communities.

In the dry season, park rangers fight wildfires.

I discovered first-hand that such firefighting is merely a holding action. During one especially dry spring, I was transfered to the night fire crew. Though our job was "grunt" work, it was exciting to be issued a bright yellow fire-retardant shirt, hard hat, and goggles. In a pickup with a pump and fire tools loaded on the back, our crew headed for the glowing flames on the darkening horizon.

The pinelands in Everglades National Park are traversed by a series of one-lane fire roads, dividing the area into blocks of a couple of thousand acres each. Our job was to patrol the perimeter of the burning pine block, making certain that the fire did not jump or creep across into an unburned zone.

Night is usually a damp, dewy time in the Everglades, so the fire was not especially active. We could see flames hopscotching through the pines, crackling with a low, flickering light. Now and then they would consume a palmetto, its dry fronds torching the night sky with a brief curtain of fire and shower of sparks.

One of the hammocks within this pine block harbored several rare species of orchids and tree snails, and flames crept uncomfortably close to its edge. The hammock was near the road, so we drove the pumper as close as possible. In the smoky glare of headlamps, we unfurled rolls of firehose through tangles of thorny greenbriar.

We saturated the edge of the hammock with a fine mist. The water sizzled and steamed as it hit the searing limestone. We were cautious where we stepped: the oven-like heat from below was capable of blistering our feet through thick boots if we stood in the wrong place too long. The hose, too, had to be checked periodically lest the underground fire flare unexpectedly and melt it.

We bathed more remote areas with water from rubberized backpacks fitted with hand pumps. Full, these "bladder bags" contained eight gallons of water—forty extra pounds hanging from our shoulders on unpadded straps. As the night dragged on, each thrashing trip with a full bag to the far side of the hammock seemed longer than the last. The return, which allowed a few moments of respite from the sloshing mini-waterbed on our backs, took no time at all. Sooty

Gnarled slash pines and jagged palmettos occupy a ridge of limestone near Florida's southeast coast.

Red-bellied woodpeckers comb furrowed slash pine bark in search of insects.

Colorful adult lubber grasshoppers roam the pinelands. Their tiny offspring are black with red stripes.

Pinelands ruellia.

and sore by morning, I was happy to trade places with the arriving day crew.

A few days later, we were recruited to a more active defense of the fire line. Wind pushed a wall of flames toward the road at the edge of a pine block. The fire boss feared sparks might jump this narrow break and wanted to widen the zone of safety. In order to do this, we would light a backing fire beside the road. Its low flames would creep slowly into the wind, toward the raging head, blackening potential fuels. By the time the main fire reached our position, the backing fire should have tripled the width of the fire break.

One member of each squad carried a canister with a diesel-gasoline mix inside. Its wick dropped flaming dribbles of fuel. Methodically the torch man ignited grass and shrubs along the edge of the road. We rushed with hand tools to douse any flare-ups outside the line. The backing fire crackled and popped into the pinelands, slowly widening the zone of burned plants.

Above the swirls of heat from our little backing fire loomed a billowing cloud of smoke from the head fire. Within minutes we could see its flames roaring through the pines toward our line. Resinous wax myrtle bushes exploded into firebrands. Vines blazed into the pine canopy, singing the feathery green needles. The air reeked with searing, screeching sighs as leaves and bark flamed, then turned to ash before our eyes.

We felt the heat of combustion on our faces, the glow now illuminating the dusky sky. The headfire met our backfire and in one stupendous moment they flared together. Just as suddenly, it was over. There was nothing left to burn. The bright glare faded to individual snags, lingering like stubborn candles on a giant birthday cake.

We scouted the nearby pine block for spot fires from sparks carried downwind. There were none. The crisis was past. The punky pine snags, their acrid smoke lingering in the stagnant air, would burn themselves out by morning.

A couple of weeks later, the spring rains began. They quenched the few remaining hot spots of these pineland fires more effectively than our best efforts with pumps and hoses. I walked through the area where the headfire raged. Its flames had gutted the land as bare as a moonscape. Only charred black trunks remained where once a diverse forest grew. It seemed unlikely that many plants or animals could have survived the conflagration.

Ten years passed before I set foot in that particular patch of pineland again. To my utter amazement, the pinelands had recovered. Grasses and low shrubs flourished here. Most of the older pines perished in the fire, but some of their sturdy cores remained standing. They were now adorned with the oval holes of pileated woodpeckers. On closer inspection, drillings in the insect-galleried wood revealed that red-bellied woodpeckers also visited frequently. Colorful lubber grasshoppers lumbered across the ground amid the purple blossoms of ruellia. Daisylike tickseed flowers waved in the breeze.

Before me spread a kaleidoscope of forest renewal. Mature trees, some near the end of their life cycle, had perished. But in their place grew sturdy young pines, many of them already head high. They flourished in a harsh world of bare rock, seasonal drought, and periodic fire. So complete were nature's recuperative powers that I doubted one visitor in a hundred, if shown this pretty little patch of pine forest, would believe that just a few years ago it lay in smoking embers.

FORESTS BORN OF THE SEA

In contrast to pine forests dependent upon periodic fires, the broad swath of coastal mangrove forest is nurtured by the sea. Fresh water that eases across mile after mile of sawgrass glades finally merges into cattail-lined creeks as it nears the Gulf and Florida Bay. Here the water surrenders its sweetness, tainted for the first time with the faint taste of salt. Here the estuaries begin.

A few miles beyond the sawgrass, networking creeks flow into broad rivers, swelled twice daily by the tides. These rivers, and even some of the meandering side creeks, are navigable by powerboat or canoe. But past their banks, deep within the jungle-gym tangle of roots that covers the floor of the mangrove forest, there are places no human being has set foot.

Patches of coastal prairie lie in scattered openings among the mangrove forests. This salt desert is marked by ground-hugging succulent plants and ghostly tree stumps. When hurricanes douse the coast, the water eventually evaporates but the salt remains. It kills trees and makes life impossible for all but the hardiest halophytes (salt-loving plants). Saltwort, glasswort, and sea purslane prosper here. To conserve precious fresh water they limit evaporation through the waxy coverings of their leaves.

Harriers cruise over the salt prairies, flushing cotton rats and seaside sparrows from their shrubby cover. One of the most common reptiles here is the diamondback rattlesnake, which reaches the enormous length of six feet in these seldom-trod coastal meadows.

Mangroves dominate, however, forming a twenty-mile-wide band that wraps the southern shore. A single red mangrove tree in shallow water resembles a long-legged spider on tiptoe, a rounded body of green perched atop thin, arching legs. In the zone where fresh water meets salt, these spidery mangroves dapple the spike rush prairies. Closer to the sea, however, mangroves grow in a wicker world of interlocking roots and branches. It is difficult to tell where one tree ends and the next begins.

Red mangroves are salt-tolerant, thriving in conditions hostile to most other trees. Beneath the tea-colored estuarine water lies pasty gray soil known as marl. Try to walk across it, and you will sink ankle deep. As you pull your feet out of the slippery soup, toes straining to hold onto your shoes, you will notice the rotten egg odor of hydrogen sulfide. There is little oxygen in this mud, and the noxious sulfur gas inhibits the growth of roots. Red mangrove's aerial roots buttress its central stalk and prop its spreading branches. Besides offering the tree multiple toeholds in the slick mud, these prop roots extract life-giving oxygen from the air when they are exposed at low tide.

Golden mangrove flowers develop into seeds that are unusual in the plant world. They are released in a "live birth" rather than as dormant nuts or acorns. Instead of falling immediately,

The freshwater glades merge into mangrove-lined creeks near the coast.

71

the fleshy seeds sprout while still attached to the parent tree. Up to ten inches long at maturity, the cigar-shaped seedlings dangle above the inhospitable marl and salt water until they have stored plenty of food reserves. Then they drop, some plunking like lawn darts into the mud beneath the parent tree. Others bob away on the tide.

Red mangrove trees line tropical shores of Africa, South and Central America, and the Pacific Islands. Their seeds are voyagers: the waxy coating and starchy cache of food inside allows them to float as long as a year before putting down roots. Thus mangroves growing side by side on the south Florida coastline may have originated from parent trees directly overhead or from seeds that drifted thousands of miles before lodging and beginning to grow.

As a mangrove seed floats, the bulbous end swells. Eventually it sinks, pulling the slender end that was once attached to the parent tree into an upright position. When the seed comes to rest on a shoal, it roots. Oval leaves burst from the top of the green cigar. Within months prop roots encircle it. The new little tree helps slow the impact of waves striking the shore. Gradually it and others growing nearby trap silt, flotsam, and leaves in their maze of intertwined roots. They stabilize the shore against the onslaught of periodic hurricanes.

Three other closely related trees grow with red mangrove in the coastal forests. Black mangrove is distinguished by masses of pencil-thin roots. These pneumatophores, or breathing tubes, extend six to eight inches above the oxygen-poor muck. Most plants cannot survive when salt water enters their systems, but black mangrove can. The tree extracts water it needs for growth from the briny tide and passes excess salt out through its leaves. Rub your finger across a black mangrove leaf, and taste the whitish bloom of salt crystals clinging to the underside.

Red and black mangrove trees will grow in salt-free environments. They are seldom found inland, though, because rival trees compete more vigorously for living space there. Mangroves are prolific along the coast because few other species can stand the salt-laden assault of wind and waves.

While black mangroves intermingle with red along the immediate coast, white mangroves usually grow on slightly higher ground farther back from shore. Buttonwood, the remaining member of the salt forest quartet, grows alongside white mangrove on these elevated banks. It is also found in coastal hammocks along with Jamaica dogwood, gumbo limbo, and mahogany. Buttonwood—named for hard, round fruits that resemble Victorian shoe buttons—has furrowed bark that provides a perfect foothold for bromeliads and butterfly orchids. At the turn of the century, old growth stands of buttonwood were cut and burned for charcoal.

The most economically important aspect of the mangrove-dominated community remains hidden from the naked eye. Beneath the rust-colored water lie tons of fallen leaves. These are the base of a complex food chain that eventually nourishes up to 90 percent of the area's sport and commercial fisheries.

Unlike trees of the temperate zone that lose their leaves in the autumn and bud out in the spring, mangrove leaves die and sprout a few at a time. Within twenty-four hours after each yellowing leaf splashes into the water, it is attacked by microscopic fungi. Once inside, these decomposers grow into a mass of thread-like filaments while they digest carbohydrates stored in the dead leaf.

Bacteria, protozoa, and other types of fungi attach to the leaf surface. To the naked eye, the blotched leaf now appears to be covered with a filmy layer of brown slime. A powerful microscope reveals the slime is actually a living mass of single-celled animals and rudimentary plants, all of which digest leaf nutrients.

Unappealing as the slime may seem, it attracts a hungry horde of flatworms, copepods, and nematodes. These minute creatures are little more than huge stomach pouches attached to eyespots and mouths. They graze on smaller plants and animals. Gradually the mangrove leaf decomposes into creature-coated detritus particles that drift with the tide. These partially digested leaf bits are now food for sea worms, marine snails, infant shrimp, and crabs.

A tangled mangrove forest dominates the coast of southern Florida.

Silvery fish called mullet, which travel through the estuaries in schools, scoop up mouthfuls of detritus-laden mud. While mullet feed directly on decomposed plant particles, most sport fish—snook, snapper, and redfish, for example—eat smaller fishes that have in turn fed on the plethora of tiny crustaceans, worms, and mollusks that digest detritus.

Energy from this complex food chain does not remain in the water. Ospreys and eagles swoop from the heavens to pluck mullet from their schools. Pelicans, cormorants, and a dozen species of wading birds gorge on the seafood banquet. Raccoons feast on coon oysters and crabs, both nourished by mangrove detritus. Even the larvae of the ubiquitous salt marsh mosquito prey upon bacteria and microbes that are basic links in the detritus food chain.

To those who have explored the coast on foot or by canoe, mangroves and mosquitoes are synonimous. Forty-three species of mosquitoes have been identified in Everglades National Park. The most numerous is the salt marsh variety, iden-tified by dark and light bands on the leg. Salt marsh mosquitoes lay eggs in the still water beneath the mangroves. Many of the hatchlings, called wigglers, are eaten by killifish and their kin. Hundreds of thousands survive. They emerge as adults about two weeks after the eggs hatch.

Mosquitoes gather in thick clouds in the mangroves and hammocks at dusk and dawn to seek mates. Most mosquitoes are weak fliers and stay within a mile of their birthplace. Pregnant salt marsh mosquitoes, however, will travel several miles in search of a blood meal. Body heat and higher carbon dioxide levels in exhaled breath, both detected at some distance, attract them. Female mosquitoes have sharp mouthparts that cut into tissue like a tiny jigsaw. They inject saliva, which causes the wound to bleed freely, then suck up blood for about ninety seconds to inject enough protein for eggs to develop. During the dry season, female mosquitoes place their eggs in the mud. The progeny lie dormant until spring rains or exceptionally high tides reflood the area.

The male mosquito, distinguished by hairy antennae, has a mouth designed to feed on plant juices or flower nectar instead of blood. The droning of his wings in your tent at night, however, can be nearly as annoying as the bite of the female. Although for short periods each summer the Arctic tundra has more mosquitoes per square foot than do the Everglades, southern Florida's mangroves are the year-round leader in mosquito production.

Each resident of Flamingo, once a fishing village and now a park visitor center amid the mangroves, has a repertoire of mosquito stories. Classics include tales of cattle, and a few people, actually killed by clouds of mosquitoes.

Early Flamingo residents discovered black mangrove smoke repelled mosquitoes. Entrances to their homes had "losers," screened rooms equipped with palm leaf fans and smoky smudge pots to drive the mosquitoes away before they entered the living area. One child who lived in Flamingo about 1910 remembers having her legs wrapped protectively in newspaper, then pulling on long pants before going outdoors. Her "playground" was a large umbrella draped with mosquito netting—the only place in the yard free enough of the insects for her to remain outdoors.

While working in the mangrove backcountry, I have been besieged by black clouds of mosquitoes more times than I care to recall. My most vivid memory, though, is of a spring night when my husband Pat and I drove to Flamingo to visit friends. Near West Lake, we heard pelting on the car's windshield and thought we had driven into a rainshower. But there were no drops. The sound was mosquitoes—millions of mosquitoes—smashing into the front of the car. We turned on the wipers for the remaining ten miles to Flamingo in order to see through the rain of tiny carcasses.

Mosquitoes are certainly not that thick all the time, and it is possible to explore the backcountry fairly easily by boat or canoe. One of the most popular destinations is Cape Sable, a shell-strewn series of beaches ten miles west of Flamingo.

Cape Sable is the southernmost reach of the United States mainland. Here ocean currents from the deeper Gulf of Mexico mingle with shallow Florida Bay. Instead of the pasty marl so common in the mangroves, waves heap bits of broken seashells onto East, Middle, and Northwest Capes. These beaches are burnished with golden sea oats that stabilize the loose shell. Rubbery-leaved railroad vine grows just above the high mark, where in summer female loggerhead turtles haul themselves ashore to deposit their precious caches of eggs. Bright red hermit crabs clump along at the surf's edge, carrying their seashell homes on their backs.

The only road that ever penetrated this part of the Everglades was completed in the early 1920s. In order to build it, fill was dredged from a ditch called the Homestead Canal dug alongside. The road was supposed to lure investors who would buy this watery paradise for vacation homes. But pesky mosquitoes, hurricanes, and the "soup-doodle" marl surface of the road did little to entice well-heeled speculators. Today the slippery road bank is overgrown with mangroves, a fading memorial to realtors' dashed dreams. The Homestead Canal provides canoeists access to Cape Sable.

Pat and I had visited East Cape on several pleasant overnight stays, so one weekend we casually decided to explore the lesser-used Middle Cape instead. After eight miles of paddling through the shady canal, we boldly bypassed the cutoff that would have channeled us into Florida Bay near East Cape. We could not know at that moment what a fateful decision we had made.

Instead we followed the Homestead Canal to the marl plug at its far end and gazed across vast Lake Ingraham. This linear estuary separates the interior mangroves from the beaches of the cape. To our amazement, the only water in the lake lay in a narrow channel that snaked through its midst. We had arrived at dead low tide. A quarter mile of soupy mud stretched between us and enough water to refloat the canoe.

If we waited the six hours for the next high tide, the sunlight of this late winter afternoon would be gone. Even if there had been enough room to pitch our tent on the plug, the mosquitoes were so abundant they would have sucked us dry by morning. We had to push on, and that

Cigar-shaped red mangrove seeds sprout while still attached to the parent tree.

Coffee bean snails crowd onto red mangrove roots at high tide. The snails are one of many links in the complex detritus food chain.

Canoeing is a popular way to explore the mangrove back country. Mosquitoes can be pesky here at times.

meant wading across the muddy shallows of Lake Ingraham as we pushed the canoe alongside.

We eased into the glop, using our paddles for stability. Warm mud gushed into our shoes. With each step, we sank — sometimes only ankle-deep, other times disappearing up to our knees. The mud made a gurgling, slurping sound as we pulled out first one foot, then the other. The smell of rotten eggs permeated the air. We howled with laughter at this ridiculous predicament.

Finally we developed a rhythm for pushing the canoe: Step-slide, slurp-slide, step-slide, slurp-slide. Half an hour later, splattered from waist to toe with putrid gray marl, we reached the channel in the midst of the lake — now only three miles to paddle to the cut that would carry us into the Gulf.

It was late afternoon by the time we reached the mouth of Lake Ingraham. Through the fifty-yard-wide cut, we could see the blue waters ahead. But the tide had turned and was now rushing in to fill the lake. We paddled into the current with all of our strength, but made no headway. The instant we rested, the canoe shot backwards.

Twice more we strained against the tide, but it was too strong. In desperation, Pat maneuvered us to the far side of the cut. We grabbed overhanging mangrove branches and pulled the canoe against the current. A shark fin sliced the water beside us. "What next?" I wondered aloud.

Two hundred yards later we had almost pulled ourselves into the Gulf. Here, however, the mangroves ended. We cast off from our last firm hold and paddled furiously. This time it worked. We reached Middle Cape in time to watch a sullen orange sun sink into the waves on the western horizon.

Already Pat was pondering the return trip. "If we head home at 8:00 AM tomorrow," he announced during supper, "we're going to hit the tides wrong again. The way I figure it, we'll need to leave here about four in the morning to reach the cut at slack tide and have enough water to cross Lake Ingraham."

So it was that we roused ourselves in the moonless predawn and paddled back along the beach until the cut materialized on the still-dark horizon. We coasted through unceremoniously, now facing the vast blackness of Lake Ingraham. Channel markers were impossible to see, so we steered by the False Cross, a bright companion constellation to the Southern Cross that marks due south here.

The air was cool and invigorating. The stars glistened overhead like diamonds on black velvet. For a time, the only sound was the dipping of our paddles and the mellow lapping of our wake against the bow of the canoe. Suddenly the stillness was broken by the rush of whirring wings. Although we could not see, we sensed a large bird approaching from the left. Instinctively we ducked as it buzzed overhead, inches above the canoe.

The day before, a flock of cormorants rested on a shoal near the channel. We surmised they were still there and the sound of our paddles aroused their curiosity. Half a dozen more times we hit the deck as low-flying cormorants barely cleared our gunwales.

Later, as the first faint glow of red licked at the eastern horizon, our pulses quickened to the yelps of a distant bobcat. Was it a male, normally a loner in these swamps, notifying females within earshot that he was available? After all, late winter is the mating season. Or was it a yearling, recently pushed out on its own, complaining that it had not been able to capture as many cotton rats and marsh rabbits among the mangrove roots as mother had been supplying? We will never know. But in both of our minds, the event became another unforgettable experience in a most memorable weekend in the mangroves.

Double-crested cormorants rest on mangrove roots.

Bobcats prowl the coastal prairies in search of cotton rats and marsh rabbits.

BEYOND THE SHORE

Despite its reputation as a River of Grass, one-third of Everglades National Park is a better home to sea turtles and bottle-nosed dolphins than to alligators. The southern and western edges of the Everglades merge into the Gulf of Mexico through shallow saltwater bays. This watery world begins where spindly red mangrove roots disappear below the surface and continues across waving pastures of submerged turtle grass.

Many of the bays—Oyster, Lostmans, and Whitewater, for example—are surrounded by mangroves. The Ten Thousand Islands, emerald isles of mangrove, dot an oyster-filled estuary near Everglades City. It is impossible to draw an exact line where the coastal forest ends and the undersea community begins.

Florida Bay is the largest body of water in the park—some twenty-five by forty miles wide. Its expansive green waters stretch beyond the horizon, filling the triangular void between the southern shore of the mainland and the upper Keys. All of these coastal estuaries are nursery grounds for a rich assortment of aquatic creatures including fish, shrimp, and crabs.

One of the shiest residents of the estuaries is the American crocodile. Although never abundant in southern Florida, this Caribbean cousin of the alligator has always found refuge in the isolated bights, or coastal bays, of eastern Florida Bay and northern Key Largo.

The crocodile's slender snout is sharply point-ed and its skin color is gray-green rather than the alligator's black. Crocs nest in sand and marl along saltwater shorelines, with females beginning to lay eggs in late April. The babies, about the same size as young alligators, hatch in late July and August. Like alligators, mother crocodiles guard their nests and help release the hatchlings.

Within their first year, about half of the ten-inch crocodile offspring fall prey to herons, raccoons, and hungry crabs. Those that survive to adulthood may reach thirty to forty years of age. Older males attain a maximum length of fifteen feet. The total U.S. population of the endangered crocodile presently stands at about 450, with more than half living in the park.

The West Indian manatee, another endangered species, frequents Whitewater Bay and lagoons along the Gulf Coast. Sea cows, as these warm-blooded creatures are also called, wander to north Florida and coastal Georgia in the summer. Chilly weather, however, pushes them to springs in central Florida and to the quiet mangrove passages of the Everglades each winter. Sea cows feed solely on aquatic vegetation, shoveling food between their bewhiskered lips with paddle-shaped flippers.

Manatees belong to a group of animals called "Sirenia," named for a vague resemblance to mermaids. They are distant kin to elephants. Should you encounter one of these docile, 1,500-pound creatures while canoeing, you have nothing to

A fascinating underwater world begins where mangrove roots disappear below the briny tide. (Photo by Pat Toops)

A crocodile, identified by its gray-green skin and slender snout, suns along the bank of the Buttonwood Canal at Flamingo.

fear. It will surface to breathe, perhaps pause to stare at you with doleful eyes, then submerge again.

Manatees have few enemies except humans in motorboats. Sea cows don't flee quickly enough to avoid collisions, and most bear deep scars on their wrinkled gray backs. About a hundred Florida manatees are known to die from boating accidents every year, a tragically high percentage for a population now estimated at only 1,200 statewide.

Bottle-nosed dolphins, on the other hand, seem to enjoy encounters with boats. They race alongside, surfing on bow wakes and jumping exuberantly. These playful mammals travel in family groups known as pods. They are excellent fish-catchers, even in the murky water of Florida Bay. To help them "see" the underwater surroundings, dolphins rely on echoing clicks emitted from their throats and blowholes. This sonar is so precise that dolphins can distinguish between the shapes of two different kinds of fish over fifty feet away.

On most days Florida Bay appears milky green near shore. The color results from sunlight being scattered by tiny bits of bay bottom lime and by diatoms, part of the floating mass of simple-celled creatures called plankton. Since the bay is so shallow—its average depth is just over four feet—wind and wave action keep these small particles suspended. Farther from shore, the water is less turbid.

One summer day, I joined Flamingo residents Hunter and Devi Sharp in exploring the underwater wonders of the bay. We motored about seven miles due south of Flamingo and anchored near Man of War Key. This small island was named for the seven-foot frigate, or man-of-war, birds that glide effortlessly overhead. We donned our snorkel masks and fins and kicked overboard into the warm, clear water.

Inches below us, ribbony blades of turtle grass undulated in the gentle current. As the name implies, the wide green leaves are nibbled by sea turtles (such as the loggerhead we spotted a few minutes earlier), as well as conchs and sea urchins. Looking carefully, we discovered thread-like pipefish swimming among the leaves. Near-by sat a small brown seahorse, its tail wrapped around a slender filament of manatee grass. This armor-plated fish outwardly resembles a knight from a chess set. It vacuums copepods and other tiny crustaceans from the grass blades through a tubelike snout.

Blue- and yellow-striped pinfish swam ahead of us. A school of perhaps three hundred silvery-sided minnows twisted and turned in unison, finally darting into the waving grasses. As we moved toward deeper water, we gazed at chimneylike bryozoans clasping the swaying stem of a sea whip and at bright red sponges clinging to chunks of limestone.

Spiny urchins littered the sea floor near the grass bed. Prickly as pincushions, these starfish relatives protect themselves with long, irritating spines. The urchin's mouth, fitted with a set of gearlike crushing teeth, is on the underside of the body.

We discovered a patch reef, marked by rounded lumps of star and brain coral. The underwater noise level at the reef increased to a constant chorus of popping and grinding. We were hearing chewing sounds as fish jaws and shrimp claws snapped shut. Hunter dove for a closer look and glimpsed a nurse shark. By the time Devi and I joined him, the shark had withdrawn into its rocky lair. All we saw was a dark round eye and the whiskered barbules on the shark's lip. These harmless creatures often lie motionless on the bottom for long periods.

On the way back to the boat, Devi and I spotted a bullet-shaped baracuda about two feet long. Although I have encountered them many times before, the baracuda's unblinking stare and gaping jaws with razor-sharp teeth made me gasp. Usually more curious than ferocious, they prey on schools of small fish, not people.

Hunter's return route led him past a spiny lobster. These oversized crayfish develop from quarter-inch floating larvae that spend their first nine months feeding in plankton mats offshore. When two inches long, the lobsters migrate to seagrass beds, where they hide by day and prowl for clams, small crabs, and sea cucumbers at night.

Had we chosen to snorkel closer to Man of War Key, the water would still have been calm, warm, and clear, but the view would have been quite different. Underwater, the mangrove roots provide a perfect point of attachment for swirling strands of filmy green algae. Among them, in Christmas wreath contrast, grow bright red fire sponges. Spidery-legged decorator crabs blend into their surroundings by sticking bits of soft coral on their shells. Jellyfish float amid the protection of the barnacle-encrusted roots. Clownish puffer fish flutter aimlessly, their spiny, bloated skin unappealing to predators such as the sleek mangrove snappers that lurk on the shadowy fringes of the key.

About a hundred keys, from the Spanish *cayo*, for "little island," stud Florida Bay. Thousands of years ago when sea levels were lower, the bay was a freshwater glade and the keys were hammocks. Now a fringe of red and black mangroves protects each island from erosive waves. Many keys have coastal prairie vegetation on their interior.

Each key is a microcosm, a self-contained world. Protected from predators such as snakes and raccoons, many of these islands are bird rookeries. Sandwich terns cluster onto keys with sandy beaches, incubating their eggs in simple depressions scraped in the broken shells. Ospreys and bald eagles balance their stick nests on hurricane-killed snags. Two or more pairs of ospreys may share larger keys, but bald eagles always lay claim to the entire island.

In contrast, wading birds such as roseate spoonbills, tricolored and little blue herons, great and snowy egrets cluster together in crowded rookeries. These nesting areas are closed to visitors because parent birds, when disturbed, squawk and flap in distress, inadvertently knocking baby birds from their flimsy nests.

As I learned when I volunteered to help band young egrets, entering a rookery is a repulsive experience. The air reverberates with the constant cries of hungry youngsters and hoarsely croaking adults. When the parent birds return from fishing, they feed their brood by retching up a paste of partially digested fish. Its oily odor

Overleaf: Manatees seek the warm, sheltered waters of Whitewater Bay and the Gulf Coast each winter.

Playful bottle-nosed dolphins race alongside boats, surfing on bow waves. (Used with permission of the Dolphin Research Center, Inc., Grassy Key, FL.)

A patch of turtlegrass with its ribbonlike leaves, shelters a juvenile blue angelfish.

blends with the sharp smell of guano from thousands of birds. The mangrove leaves are whitewashed with this excrement, and after a while, so are bird banders. Maggot-infested carcasses of youngsters that were pushed or toppled from the nests lie beneath the trees. How ironic it is that birds we consider so beautiful and graceful begin life in conditions most humans would categorize as squalid.

Parents seldom fly far to feed. At low tide only a skim of water remains in the bays and lagoons. Fish are abundant and easy to stab. Fiddler crabs wander out of their burrows and across the exposed mudflats. Their name refers to the enlarged claw that males wave during courtship. At times great armies of these three-inch crabs creep across the soggy mud. Many fall victim to stalking yellow-crowned night herons and stately great white herons.

The great white heron, which stands three feet tall and has a wingspan twice that length, is a resident of south Florida's coastal corridor. The great white is technically a color form of the great blue heron, but John James Audubon first described it as a separate species in the 1830s. He was amazed by the heron's voracious appetite. Although great whites normally eat oily sardines, thread herring, and mullet, they do occasionally kill and eat birds nearly half their size.

Great whites are themselves tasty, and in years past they appeared on many a dinner table in the Keys. With great white heron numbers already low, a 1935 hurricane nearly wiped out the remainder. When the winds subsided, only 146 of the huge herons could be found. Protection of their roosts and rookeries, however, allowed the population to increase to the present two thousand.

Brown pelicans flourish on a diet of estuarine fish. The homely birds dive head-first into the bays. When they bob back to the surface, their expandable throat pouches are swollen with food and as much as two gallons of water. So pelicans contract the elastic throat skin, squeezing out the water and finally swallowing just the fish. When not feeding, pelicans rest among the mangrove branches. The species, once endangered by DDT-based pesticides, is now abundant along the Florida coasts.

The Everglades estuaries change subtly from moment to moment and season to season. Wind and tide stir a constant interchange between mainland runoff and the saline waters of the Gulf. Underwater, fish, crabs, and shrimp migrate from grass beds to prop-root-lined creeks and back again as they play out the drama of their life cycles.

Sandpipers patter at the edge of the water, where seafoam laps at the muddy banks. Magnificent wading birds shuffle through the shallows, marking the ebb and flow of the tide by their distance from shore. At sunset a flight of egrets lifts into the air. Their hunger finally satisfied, the graceful birds head for another secure night at an offshore roost. It is here, in an everchanging setting of wind, water, and wildlife, that the Everglades reach their outermost limit.

Once endangered by pesticides, brown pelicans are now abundant along Florida's coasts.

The brown anole, introduced from Cuba, is established in many Everglades hammocks.

STABILITY AND CHANGE

From sawgrass to bayshore, the Everglades harbor a beautifully sequenced progression of life. Plants and animals within the glade, hammock, pineland, and mangrove communities interact among themselves and with their neighbors. Through centuries of coexistence, each species has settled into a comfortable niche, a home that provides the necessities of life. Instinctively these animals and plants struggle to hold their places against the competition of all others.

Within nature's scheme, the forces of change are constantly at work. Not too many thousands of years ago, salty Florida Bay was a sweet sawgrass glade. Over time, rainbow-hued tree snails have diversified from a common Caribbean ancestor. These natural changes occur slowly on the scale of geological time. Under human influence, however, changes can be much more rapid. One century ago, could anyone have dared to imagine the frighteningly fast pace of development in south Florida today? Would newspaperman A. P. Williams of the *Times-Democrat* expedition have believed the network of roads and canals that cross his "vast and useless marsh"?

Even though certain sections of the Everglades are seldom visited, they are not so remote as to be unaffected by human actions. The region is no longer the unbroken wilderness that once stretched from Lake Okeechobee to the sea. Wading birds have dwindled from hundreds of thousands to flocks a tenth that size. The Everglades face serious threats from exotic plant and animal invaders.

Schinus, a scarlet-berried bush from Brazil, and paperbarked Australian *Melaleuca* were imported as landscaping shrubbery. Both prolific seeders, they have escaped from cultivation and spread rampantly. So far undaunted by the natural checks of fire or drought, they are crowding out native vegetation at an alarming rate.

Walking catfish and talapia, both imported for the aquarium trade, have made their way from accidental releases into city canals to the heart of Everglades sloughs. They prey upon the eggs and fingerlings of native fish and are now so widespread they are unlikely ever to be eradicated.

From fire ants to mynah birds, the list of aggressive species relocated into south Florida from the worldwide tropics grows. Some find favorable conditions and few natural enemies. Their populations expand unchecked. This "biological fallout" may change the face of the region permanently.

Or will it? The Everglades exist in a regime of pulse stability. Cycles of flood and drought, fires, and hurricanes shape the landscape. The Everglades persist amid change. Plant and animal residents must cope with wild swings from wet to dry and back again. Some of the invaders will outcompete the natives. Others will eventually bow to one of the swings of the biological pendulum.

This swinging pendulum has traditionally

Bright red berries of Brazilian pepper (Schinus) are eaten by songbirds. The shrub has escaped from cultivation into remote hammocks, pinelands, and mangrove forests.

created a cushioning effect for the native plants and animals. No one set of conditions favors all Everglades species. Apple snails and snail kites do well in times of flood, but wood storks do not. Pinelands proliferate in the same fires that destroy hammocks. Everglades diversity is preserved by the interplay of wet versus dry, favoring first one community, then another over a cycle of several years.

Pessimists label the Everglades "fragile." They compare the region to a fine porcelain vase. The vase is teetering at the edge of the mantlepiece, they say. When it falls, it will shatter and nothing but mismatched pieces will remain.

Optimists see the resiliency of the Everglades. They draw parallels with the resurrection fern that grows on live oak branches in the hammocks. During summer rains or when abundant humidity bathes the air, the fern flourishes. In dry times, however, the leaves shrink into crisp

brown curls. Far from death, they are merely conserving energy and waiting. When another wet period arrives, they unfurl and continue luxuriant growth. So, too, do Everglades species survive the droughts and reproduce in the times of abundance.

Naturalist Charles Torey Simpson complained that south Florida was being destroyed—its hammocks leveled, glades drained, pine forests cut for timber, and wildlife becoming rare. His words were published in 1920. Nearly seventy years later, fine examples of sawgrass marsh, tree islands, and pine forests remain within Everglades National Park and Big Cypress Preserve. Here a few panthers still roam and wood storks hang on to a semblance of their former life. Given a chance, nature maintains itself against sometimes overwhelming adversity.

Natural areas have always been sacrificed or compromised, and the Everglades are no excep-

Among the most colorful of the region's residents is the purple gallinule.

tion. Pinelands and hammocks, orchids and tree snails have fallen at the doorsteps of millions of new Florida residents. Alligator holes go dry at times so that Gold Coast residents may have the 300 billion gallons of water a day that flow into homes and onto agricultural fields.

We continue to satisfy our taste for ripe tomatoes and strawberries in the middle of winter, never mind that fewer wading birds find suitable areas to feed and nest. These trade-offs should not surprise us, for we are part of nature rather than apart from it. We shape the Everglades of the future.

Considering all the adversity surrounding the Everglades, it is a marvel that such a wellspring of wildlife survives. The Florida Everglades are the last refuge for several threatened plants and animals. Scientists still have much to learn about Everglades species. It is entirely possible that a few will disappear before the intricacies of their life cycles are discovered. Our planet will be a poorer place if they are lost, and all who feel themselves a part of nature will mourn their passing.

From shady hammock to sunny glade, from ancient pine ridge to peat still building beneath the mangrove roots, this is a land of contrasts and curiosities. The Everglades are complex and diverse. They are a place of concern and of hope.

Each evening, when the sun's crimson glow fades from the western sky and the stars begin to sparkle, there is a quiet sense of expectation among visitors and residents alike. The following day will most certainly dawn new and bright over a place with no equal on earth. It will illuminate an ever-changing, yet in some respects, never-changing landscape known simply as the Everglades.

Hurricane Andrew, the region's most powerful storm in the previous half-century, struck Everglades National Park on August 24, 1992, leaving a jumble of uprooted trees and broken branches.

HURRICANE ANDREW

Sunday, August 23, 1992, was a deceptively beautiful day in south Florida. If not for the periodic warnings on local radio and television stations, few would have guessed of an approaching storm.

Around 5 A.M. the next day, Hurricane Andrew slashed into Biscayne National Park with wind gusts exceeding 160 miles per hour. Andrew was Florida's strongest hurricane in the previous half-century. A compact, fast-moving storm, it cut a 25-mile-wide swath west across Dade County. Terror-struck families from Coral Gables to Homestead huddled in bathrooms or crowded into closets as their homes disintegrated into the shrieking winds.

The main body of Hurricane Andrew crossed Everglades National Park from Chekika Hammock on the north to the Anhinga Trail and Pa-hay-okee on the south, then swirled west to the Broad and Lostmans Rivers. Winds near the eye snapped slash pines like match sticks, flattened hardwood hammocks, and toppled mangroves in the storm's path. By 8 A.M. the hurricane blew into the Gulf of Mexico, leaving a jumbled landscape of fallen trees, leafless branches, and mangled structures.

While south Florida's human residents struggled

Although evidence of Hurricane Andrew will persist for years, lush new growth on hurricane-adapted species, such as gumbo limbo, is rapidly restoring a shady canopy to the region's hammocks.

to rebuild their lives and park officials labored to repair visitor facilities, native flora and fauna rebounded with amazing vitality. Almost immediately after the storm, tree snails roamed the rain-dampened trunks, grazing on algae nourished by new patches of sunlight. Within ten days, fig, wild tamarind, and gumbo limbo trees pushed out fresh sets of leaves. Deer, wading birds, and alligators continued to roam the marshes, apparently unaffected. The overwash of new sand on several wilderness beaches has actually improved conditions for nesting sea turtles and crocodiles. However, uprooted hardwood hammocks and coastal mangrove forests did provide new footholds for exotic *Schinus, Melaleuca,* and *Casuarina* trees, which are a continuing threat to the native ecosystem.

Evidence of Hurricane Andrew will persist for some years to come. As with memorable predecessors—Hurricane Donna, which ravaged Flamingo in 1960, and the Labor Day Hurricane of 1935—Andrew's wind-borne mayhem will gradually heal. Natural cycles, with their associated growth and death, will continue to reshape the face of the Everglades landscape as they have for eons.

THE EVERGLADES ECOSYSTEM

Everglades National Park's golden anniversary offers an opportunity to reflect on south Florida's ecological health. During the past half-century, the United Nations Educational, Scientific, and Cultural Organization (UNESCO) designated the park an International Biosphere Reserve and a World Heritage Site. The Everglades is also a Wetland of International Significance. But a study conducted recently by the Defenders of Wildlife concluded south Florida has the most endangered ecosystem in the nation. Wading bird populations continue to dwindle and the once-sparkling waters of Florida Bay are fouled. One out of every hundred species of plants and animals native to Everglades National Park is considered endangered by the state of Florida or by the U.S. Fish and Wildlife Service. Among these are American crocodiles, loggerhead sea turtles, snail kites, wood storks, Florida panthers, and Florida royal palm trees.

It is not possible to pinpoint an individual catastrophic event responsible for the decline of south Florida's ecosystem. In a region so biologically diverse, the health of each species depends upon many intertwined relationships. What negatively affects one plant or animal can have a rippling effect along the food chain. This is particularly evident in the case of Florida panthers.

Only thirty or so of the big cats remain statewide, most of them living elusively in the Big Cypress. The last native female panther in Everglades National Park, an animal which resided in the Long Pine Key area, died in 1991. Though half of the state's panther deaths during the previous decade resulted from highway collisions, and special panther crossings have been installed in high traffic areas to reduce this threat, the Florida panther faces another impending danger from something more ominous: mercury poisoning.

Female panthers often hunt large prey—usually whitetailed deer—to provide enough food to raise cubs. But if deer are scarce, panthers feed on smaller fare such as raccoons, otters, and young alligators. These prey species, in turn, dine on fish from Everglades marshes. The fish are tainted with mercury. Necropsies of dead Everglades panthers revealed abnormally high concentrations of mercury in several of their livers. Similar levels of mercury poisoning in humans can affect the central nervous system or damage brain cells, causing loss of coordination, vision problems, blindness, or death.

Mercury can be detected in the rain that falls on south Florida and is transformed by naturally-occurring bacteria into compounds the fish ingest. Some of the mercury has been traced to regional power

Like many plants and animals of the Everglades, the Julia butterfly is native to the tropics. In the United States, Julias occur only in southern Florida and Texas.

Mercury moves up the food chain from tiny aquatic creatures, through fish, raccoons, and alligators, to panthers and humans. Abnormally high levels of mercury have been found in the tissue of dead Florida panthers.

plants and medical waste incinerators. Other sources of mercury are global, coming from industrial emissions—perhaps from as far away as China—that are dispersed into upper levels of the atmosphere.

In the past century, mercury has been widely used in paints, batteries, fluorescent light bulbs, cosmetics, and medical products. This potentially toxic heavy metal is three times more common in the environment now than it was a hundred years ago. Fortunately, the detrimental effects of mercury in ecosystems such as the Everglades have precipitated a number of research projects and tougher laws. Mercury usage in paints, batteries, and inks has decreased. In Florida, the recycling of products such as fluorescent bulbs is now common. Tougher pollution laws are lowering emissions from incinerators and power plants. But similar actions will be needed on a worldwide scale to significantly reduce mercury levels in the Ever-

glades ecosystem.

While mercury pollution is a serious problem in the Everglades, the human population explosion in south Florida is an even greater concern. The Everglades is a shrinking island of wildness surrounded by an ever-increasing number of people. Mosquito reduction, flood control, and air conditioning have made living in south Florida a pleasant proposition. The state's population is growing at twice the national average, with five million current residents in the Everglades region. Planners estimate 6.2 million people will reside there by 2015. Each new resident consumes a little more clean water and requires a little more living space.

This "nibbling degradation" is hard to fight. Pinelands and hardwood hammocks have disappeared a few new city blocks at a time. Suburbs are creeping into the marshes. Each act seems fairly insignificant by itself, but when the acts are combined, the results are staggering. Half of the original Florida Everglades are now drained. They are being smothered by urban sprawl, air pollution, poorly treated sewage, and agricultural byproducts. For those who knew the park in its heyday, the current situation is heartbreaking.

Unfortunately, symptoms of the Everglades' ill health are much more obvious than any path to a cure. It is unrealistic to expect that the millions of people who now live in south Florida will leave. A more relevant question is, can the human population learn how to live in harmony with the remaining natural areas?

Despite a century of abuse, many viable components of the once-great Everglades survive. It is possible to preserve for future generations a semblance of the Everglades our forebears knew. Years ago hydrologists targeted water use to specific human needs. Recently, ecologists and resource managers from various federal, state, and local jurisdictions have started to regard the Everglades as a multifaceted wetland system that encompasses the southern half of the Florida peninsula. They are realizing that what happens in the Kissimmee Basin, Lake Okeechobee, or the River of Grass affects the entire ecosystem. Among their goals are protecting the remaining mosaic of natural habitat and providing greenways to reconnect fragmented areas.

Spurred by several conservation organizations,

The human population explosion in south Florida is one of the greatest threats to the Everglades ecosystem. In the past century, Dade County's population has increased from one thousand to two million residents.

In order to restore the water quality and quantity necessary to revitalize the Everglades, south Florida's canal system is being reconfigured to mimic historic rainfall patterns.

Florida's voters and lawmakers have vowed to restore the water quality and quantity needed to revitalize the Everglades. Their plan includes reconfigurations of south Florida's canal system to mimic historic rainfall-based patterns in their timing and delivery of water. Planning, acquiring land, and physically restoring surface water, however, is a slow process. Also, the question of what is "normal" is hard to define in a system that has undergone such radical change. But the effort to un-tame south Florida is proceeding.

Approximately $400 million will be spent over fifteen years to restore the meanders, groundwater recharge, and wildlife habitat along the Kissimmee River between Orlando and Lake Okeechobee. An additional 107,600 acres of wetland habitat are being added to Everglades National Park. Adjustments in water management will increase surface flows to Shark and Taylor sloughs. More water coursing through Taylor Slough should help reduce the abnormally high salinity of eastern Florida Bay.

There is more good news. Back in the 1970s, an inholding of about 9,000 acres of farmland known as the "Hole-in-the-Donut" was added to Everglades National Park. Farm fertilizers and pesticides were leaching into the groundwater and were suspected to be hampering the reproduction of bald eagles and ospreys. When farming ceased, chemical pollution decreased. But the disturbed soils became a seedbed for invading Brazilian pepper (*Schinus*) trees. Over the years, managers experimented with mowing, burning, and bulldozing the fields. They planted native grasses, pines, and tropical hardwoods. They also applied various herbicides in an effort to kill the pesky alien trees, but to no avail. The former farmlands grew into an impenetrable thicket of Brazilian pepper trees that served as a seed source to infect surrounding stands of native pines.

Alert Everglades managers noted, however, that in one wet area where soil had been scraped off the underlying limestone, no pepper trees grew. A few years ago they removed all of the seed-contaminated soil from another test plot and allowed seasonal flooding to cover the resulting bare rock. The area reverted to a typical wetland, with sawgrass, muhly grass, and a variety of native herbs seeding in from the surrounding glades. Standing water killed the Brazilian pepper seedlings.

A Dade County law is also helping to eliminate these red-fruited invaders. Developers who build on wetland sites must restore an equal area of wetland or contribute to a mitigation trust fund. Everglades managers are now applying money from this fund to rehabilitate about 250 acres of former "Donut" farmland annually. They hope to wipe out Brazilian pepper trees and return native plants to this portion of the park within the next two decades.

After years of aggressively cutting and treating *Melaleuca* trees with herbicides in the Big Cypress, the managers are finally making headway in ridding the preserve of this exotic species. They have also undertaken restoration of the Turner River, a meandering stream that flows into the mangrove swamps in the northwestern corner of Everglades National

Facing page: Resource managers have recently discovered that bulldozing exotic Brazilian pepper trees and removing the seed-laden soil down to the bedrock creates an environment in which native plants will seed back into Everglades marshes. Above: Swamp lobelia is one of the native wildflowers now growing in the rehabilitated area.

Several decades ago, chemicals such as DDT caused osprey populations to decline. These fish-eating hawks are now a common sight along Florida's coasts.

Park. In the 1960s several roads were built by dredging canals and using the fill for roadbeds. The canals drained water from the surrounding marsh. Salt water intruded, the old river bed became clogged with vegetation, and freshwater fish populations declined.

Using funding from wetlands violation fines and from Florida's "Save Our Everglades" program (an initiative spearheaded by former Governor Bob Graham), workers placed a number of culverts under the roads. They plugged the canal with a series of small earthen dams and rock fill. This is forcing water back into the marshes. Although not completely pristine, the restored Turner River provides improved wetland habitat and has become a popular wildlife observation area for park visitors. Similar plans will be used to plug other canals in the region.

Several animals whose populations were shrinking are now recovering. Ospreys and bald eagles, threatened a few decades ago because the fish they ate were laced with DDT and other pesticides that caused their egg shells to break, have once more achieved stable numbers. American alligators, formerly threatened by poaching, have been removed from endangered status. American crocodile and snail kite populations are also slowly increasing.

Environmental education coordinator Sandy Dayhoff, who has lived in the Big Cypress since she was sixteen, remembers a day years ago when she saw her first snail kite. She was with Erwin Winte, one of Everglades National Park's first rangers. "Erwin got so excited," she recalled. "There were only thirty-six pairs of kites in all of south Florida then. Now it's not unusual to see them at Shark Valley." At one time, only twenty-five of these birds remained in the state. About fifteen hundred snail kites presently inhabit Florida.

Sandy has spent lots of time at Shark Valley during her Park Service career. For more than a quarter-century she has been instrumental in Everglades National Park's education program, which brings fourth grade students from Dade, Broward, Collier, Monroe, Lee, and Hendry counties to spend a day in the park. Many graduates of the day program come back as fifth or sixth graders for a three-day camping experience at the Loop Road Education Center in Big Cypress National Preserve or at the Hidden Lake Education Center in Everglades National Park.

On visits to the park, students from elementary schools in south Florida learn first-hand about the Everglades ecosystem.

Although teachers present extensive pre-visit lessons, this is the real thing—wet feet, mosquitoes, alligators, cute green frogs in the bathrooms, and weird sounds at night. A majority of the children have never been to the Everglades, even though the park is less than fifty miles from most of their homes. As they trek into the marsh on a slough slog, they realize the Everglades is very different from their city environment.

Teachers and rangers help excited students spot alligators, turtles, and birds. The students play games that involve predator-prey relationships and howl with laughter when rangers arrive at evening campfires dressed as spiders or wood storks. In truth, the kids are having such a great time they seldom realize they are learning about ecology and hydrology.

Graphic activities, such as "Sponging Off The Everglades," offer lasting impressions. A ranger fills a sponge with water from the marsh and tells the kids this represents the Biscayne Aquifer, which supplies water for all of south Florida. Ten students are selected to tell the group how they use water. "Brushing teeth … flushing toilets … drinking … washing cars," they say. With each answer the ranger squeezes a bit of water from the sponge. Finally one of the children remembers the Everglades need water, too. "Too bad," says the ranger, squeezing hard. "Only a few drops left."

Neil De Jong began working with the environmental education program nearly twenty years ago and is now the park's chief of interpretation. He explains "Judgment Day," an activity he believes is one of the most memorable aspects of student campouts. On the last day, groups of campers are assigned roles: farmers, developers, tourists, and conservationists. The students receive symbols of their assigned causes to wear—such as a hard hat or an alligator's nose—then they act out their roles before a panel of judges, played by their teachers and chaperones. "We tell them there is only so much water available," De Jong explained, "and everyone gets some." Throughout the program, the children hear the theme "Together we work toward the future of the Everglades." Not only do they use it to present impassioned cases on judgment day, said De Jong, but teachers report the debate sometimes goes on for several weeks once they return to class.

During the past twenty-six years, the education program has brought a quarter of a million area school children to the Everglades. Is it making a difference? Some of the students contribute simple acts to help the Everglades, such as conserving water when they brush their teeth or reporting leaky faucets. For others, the visit is life changing. Children inspired by their trip to the Everglades have grown up to be teachers or chaperones who bring new generations to the park. Others have become park rangers, marine biologists, artists whose work is displayed in park visitor centers, or members of community zoning boards. The enthusiasm of the children also spreads to their parents, who may begin to take more interest in conservation issues.

Despite the many positive aspects of the education program, the enormity of the threats facing the Everglades ecosystem is quite daunting. "Sometimes, as I look into the bright eyes of these kids, and I see such excitement and hope," Sandy Dayhoff reflected, "I

Facing page: Mist rises from a pond near Parachute Key at dawn. Above: When they show creatures such as this black-and-yellow argiope spider to visitors, park rangers often recall the words of Chief Seattle: "Man did not weave the web of life; he is merely a strand in it. Whatever he does to the web, he does to himself."

wonder what will be here when they grow up."

"I think we make a difference—maybe a very subtle difference, like the place we teach about," she continued. "I see more environmental awareness. People want to help, they just don't always know how."

Among the best rewards of her job are moments when a parent stops to chat after a program and says, "I've lived here all my life, and I always thought of the Everglades as a wasteland. You've changed my whole perspective."

There's an adage that claims if you don't understand something, you won't appreciate and protect it. Perhaps the best hope for the Everglades is this new generation of young Floridians. They are beginning to realize how important it is to coexist in harmony with the natural treasure that lies just beyond their backyards.

SELECTED PARKS AND PRESERVES IN THE EVERGLADES REGION

Arthur R. Marshall Loxahatchee National Wildlife Refuge
10216 Lee Road
Boynton Beach, FL 33437
(561) 734-8303

Big Cypress National Preserve
HCR 61, Box 11
Ochopee, FL 34141
(941) 695-4111

Biscayne Bay Aquatic Preserve
Card Sound Aquatic Preserve
Coupon Bight Aquatic Preserve
Lignumvitae Key Aquatic Preserve
2796 Overseas Highway, Suite 218
Marathon, FL 33050
(305) 289-2336

Biscayne National Park
P.O. Box 1369
Homestead, FL 33090-1369
(305) 230-7275

Collier Seminole State Park
20200 East Tamiami Trail
Naples, FL 34114
(941) 394-3397

Corkscrew Swamp Sanctuary
375 Sanctuary Road
Naples, FL 34120
(941) 657-3771

Crocodile Lake National Wildlife Refuge
P.O. Box 370
Key Largo, FL 33037
(305) 451-4223

Dry Tortugas National Park
P.O. Box 6208
Key West, FL 33041
(305) 242-7700 [The Everglades National Park office at this number provides information on Dry Tortugas National Park]

Everglades National Park
40001 State Road 9336
Homestead, FL 33034-6733
(305) 242-7700

Fakahatchee Strand State Preserve
P.O. Box 548
Copeland, FL 34137
(941) 695-4593

Florida Keys National Marine Sanctuary
P.O. Box 1083
Key Largo, FL 33037
(305) 852-7717

Florida Panther National Wildlife Refuge
Ten Thousand Islands National Wildlife Refuge
3860 Tollgate Boulevard, Suite 300
Naples, FL 34114
(941) 353-8442

J.N. "Ding" Darling National Wildlife Refuge
1 Wildlife Drive
Sanibel, FL 33957
(941) 472-1100

John Pennekamp Coral Reef State Park
Key Largo Hammock State Botanical Site
P.O. Box 487
Key Largo, FL 33037
(305) 451-1202

Indian Key State Historic Site
Lignumvitae Key State Botanical Site
San Pedro Underwater Archeological Preserve
Windley Key Fossil Reef State Geological Site
P.O. Box 1052
Islamorada, FL 33036
(305) 664-4815

Picayune Strand State Forest
710 Randall Blvd.
Naples, FL 34120
(941) 352-4212

ENVIRONMENTAL ORGANIZATIONS INVOLVED IN EVERGLADES ISSUES

Biscayne Bay Foundation
1024 Almeria Avenue
Coral Gables, FL 33134
(305) 447-4566

Founded in 1996, the Foundation promotes greater appreciation and understanding of the Biscayne Bay ecosystem and Biscayne National Park. Members represent a broad spectrum of scientists, community activists, urban planners, small business owners, lawyers, and others who consider Biscayne Bay an important part of south Florida's heritage and bounty. They participate in bay advocacy and land use planning, water quality monitoring, exotic species removal, bay and reef cleanups, and civic events. The group also partners with Biscayne National Park and the Dade County Public Schools in a "Parks as Classrooms" program for fourth and fifth grade students.

The Conservancy of Southwest Florida
1450 Merrihue Drive
Naples, FL 34102
(941) 262-0304

The Conservancy is a nonprofit organization active in protecting and sustaining southwestern Florida's native ecosystems. The group was organized in 1964 to save 2,600 acres of pineland, mangrove, and estuarine habitat in Rookery Bay from development. Since then, the Conservancy has protected some

300,000 additional acres of environmentally sensitive land in the region. The Conservancy operates the Naples Nature Center and the Wildlife Rehabilitation Center in Naples. It also maintains the Briggs Nature Center in the Rookery Bay National Estuarine Research Reserve.

Everglades Ecosystem Restoration Campaign
c/o National Audubon Society
444 Brickell Avenue, Suite 850
Miami, FL 33131
(305) 371-6399

The National Audubon Society came into existence a century ago to protect the wading birds of the Everglades region. The Society has maintained an active presence in south Florida through scientific research and sanctuary acquisitions. In 1992 the National Audubon Society began a major program of scientific research, policy recommendations, grassroots activism, and public education to restore the Everglades ecosystem. At present, Audubon is the largest nonprofit organization active in this restoration effort.

Florida National Parks & Monuments Association

10 Parachute Key, #51
Homestead, FL 33034-6735
(305) 247-1216

The Florida National Parks & Monuments Association is a nonprofit organization working with the National Park Service to assist visitors to Everglades, Biscayne, and Dry Tortugas National Parks and Big Cypress National Preserve. The organization publishes park-specific books and operates bookstores in park visitor centers. It offers a wide range of publications, videos, maps, and other educational materials relating to the flora, fauna, and history of southern Florida. Proceeds from bookstore sales are returned to the parks to support educational, scientific, historical, and visitor service programs, such as providing checklists of wildlife species likely to be seen in the park and a newspaper that reports on park activities.

Florida Panther Recovery Fund

c/o National Fish & Wildlife Foundation
1120 Connecticut Avenue, NW Suite 900
Washington, D.C. 20036
(202) 857-0166

The National Fish & Wildlife Foundation is a nonprofit organization established by Congress in 1984 to conserve natural resources through habitat restoration, resource management, environmental education, and public policy development. The agency bestows challenge grants, funded by matching federal and private appropriations. It administers the Florida Panther Recovery Fund, which accepts donations to further panther research and recovery.

Friends of the Everglades

7800 Red Road, Suite 215K
Miami, FL 33143
(305) 669-0858

In 1969 Marjory Stoneman Douglas, author of *The Everglades: River of Grass*, joined several prominent environmentalists in a campaign to stop a regional jetport from being built in the Big Cypress Swamp. The group was successful and has continued with its mission of protecting and preserving the Everglades region through education, public policy, and advocacy. Friends of the Everglades currently numbers about six thousand volunteer members.

South Florida/Everglades Campaign

c/o World Wildlife Fund
1250 24th Street NW
Washington, D.C. 20036-1175
(202) 293-4800

World Wildlife Fund is an international conservation agency that also focuses on selected domestic issues to preserve the abundance and diversity of life on earth. The organization administers a major campaign to restore the health of the Everglades ecosystem.

Tropical Audubon Society

5530 Sunset Drive
Miami, FL 33143
(305) 666-5111

The office of the Miami chapter of the National Audubon Society preserves a historic home in South Miami and features landscaping with native plants of the Keys and hammocks. Tropical Audubon Society maintains an extensive library on the birds of southern Florida and provides information on south Florida's endangered species. The group is currently working to emphasize responsible ecotourism and sustainable tropical agriculture in the area.

Young Friends of the Everglades

7800 Red Road, Suite 215K
Miami, FL 33143
(305) 669-0858

Students and teachers at Howard Drive Elementary school in Miami organized Young Friends of the Everglades in 1994. The young people wanted a more active voice in their future natural heritage. Club members promote preservation of the Everglades by writing letters, offering input at political meetings, and publishing a newsletter. They also participate in activities such as tree plantings and field trips. The group focuses on upper elementary school children but is open to all ages.

BIBLIOGRAPHY

Atkeson, Tom (Mercury Project Coordinator, Florida Department of Environmental Protection). Telephone conversation with author, 20 June 1997.

Beard, Daniel B. *Special Report: Everglades National Park Project*. Washington, D.C.: National Park Service, 1938.

Bell, C. Ritchie, and Bryan J. Taylor. *Florida Wild Flowers and Roadside Plants*. Chapel Hill, N.C.: Laurel Hill Press, 1982.

Carr, Archie. *The Everglades*. New York: Time-Life Books, 1973.

Caulfield, Patricia. *Everglades*. San Francisco: Sierra Club, 1970.

Davidson, Treat. "Tree Snails, Gems of the Everglades." *National Geographic*, 127 (March 1965): 372–387.

de Golia, Jack. *Everglades: The Story Behind the Scenery*. Las Vegas: KC Publications, 1978.

Douglas, Marjory Stoneman. *The Everglades: River of Grass*. Marietta, Ga.: Mockingbird Books, 1947.

Fitzgerald, William, and Thomas W. Clarkson. "Mercury and Monomethylmercury: Present and Future Concerns." *Environmental Health Perspectives,* 96 (1991): 159–166.

George, Jean Craighead. *Everglades Wildguide*, 3rd ed. Washington, D.C.: National Park Service/Government Printing Office, 1997.

Governor's Commission for a Sustainable South Florida. *A Conceptual Plan for the Central and Southern Florida Project Restudy*. Tallahassee: Florida Department of Community Affairs, Florida Coastal Management Program, 1996.

Hansen, Kevin. "South Florida's Water Dilemma," *Environment* 26 (June 1984): 14–20, 39–42.

Hawkes, Alex D. *Guide to Plants of the Everglades National Park*. Coral Gables, Fla.: Tropic Isle Publishers, 1965.

Hoffmeister, John Edward. *Land from the Sea: The Geologic Story of South Florida*. Coral Gables, Fla.: University of Miami Press, 1974.

Jones, A. Durand. *Mercury Contamination in Wildlife*. Homestead, Fla.: National Park Service, 1991.

Mairson, Alan. "The Everglades: Dying for Help." *National Geographic* 185 (April 1994): 2–35.

Robertson, William B., Jr. *Everglades: The Park Story*, 2d ed. Homestead, Fla.: Florida National Parks and Monuments Association, Inc., 1989.

Stevenson, George B. *Trees of Everglades National Park and the Florida Keys*, 2d ed. Homestead, Fla.: Florida National Parks and Monuments Association, 1992.

Taylor, Caroline. *Restoring the River of Grass*. Miami: National Audubon Society, 1996.

Tebeau, Charlton W. *Man in the Everglades*, 2d ed. Coral Gables, Fla.: University of Miami Press, 1968.

Toops, Connie. *The Alligator: Monarch of the Marsh*, 2d ed. Homestead, Fla.: Florida National Parks & Monuments Association, 1988.

———. "The Florida Panther." In *Insight Guide: U.S. National Parks East*, edited by John Gattuso. London: APA Publications Ltd., 1995.

Toops, Connie, and Willard E. Dilley. *Birds of South Florida*. Conway, Ark.: River Road Press, 1986.

INDEX

(Photo by Pat Toops)

ABOUT THE AUTHOR

Connie Toops, who grew up in Covington, Ohio, has always been fascinated with nature. She earned a Bachelor of Science degree in natural resources from Ohio State University in 1972. While in college, she worked as a naturalist in the Ohio state park system and in Colonial, Rocky Mountain, and Shenandoah National Parks. After graduation, she continued working as a naturalist and ranger at Shenandoah, Crater Lake, and Everglades National Parks.

As a freelance photojournalist, Connie has returned to the Everglades numerous times. Her photos have graced Audubon and Sierra Club calendars and books published by National Geographic, Sierra Club, Reader's Digest, Time-Life, and Voyageur Press. She has written nine nature books for adults, including four other Voyageur Press titles: *Bluebirds Forever, Hummingbirds: Jewels in Flight, Owls,* and *Great Smoky Mountains.* She has developed the *Let's Explore* series of children's nature activity guides and writes articles that appear regularly in conservation magazines.

Connie and her husband Pat, a resource management specialist for the National Park Service, have lived in or near eight national parks and monuments during the past two decades. They share a love of birding, canoeing, and travel to natural areas throughout the world. They currently make their home in Martinsburg, West Virginia, where they have converted a suburban half-acre into a mini wildlife refuge.